*sirocco

sirocco

Fabulous flavours from the East

Sabrina Ghayour

Photography by Haarala Hamilton

MITCHELL BEAZLEY

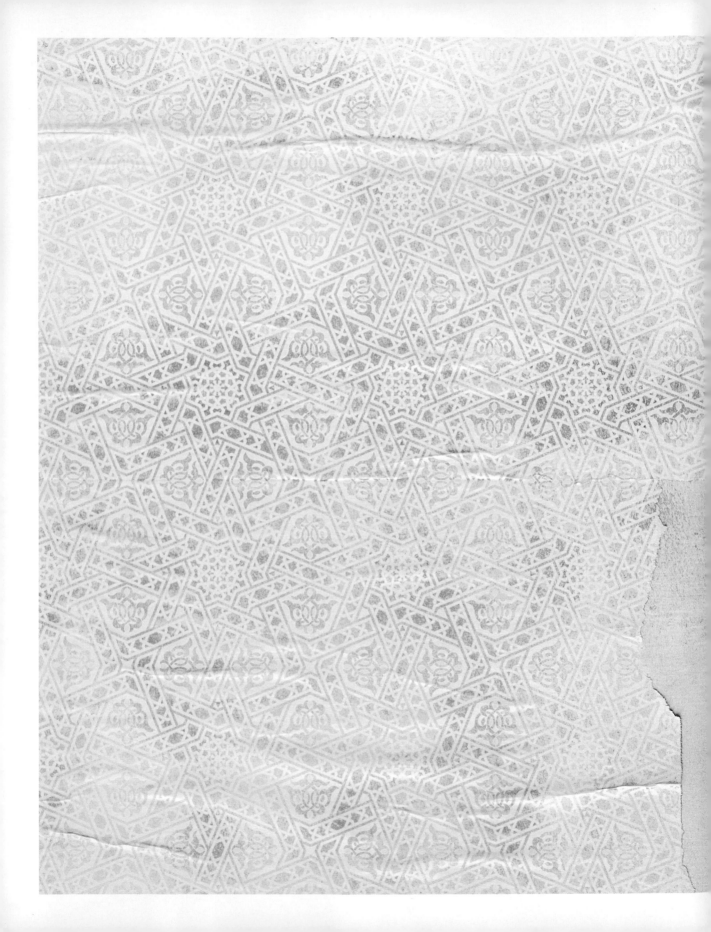

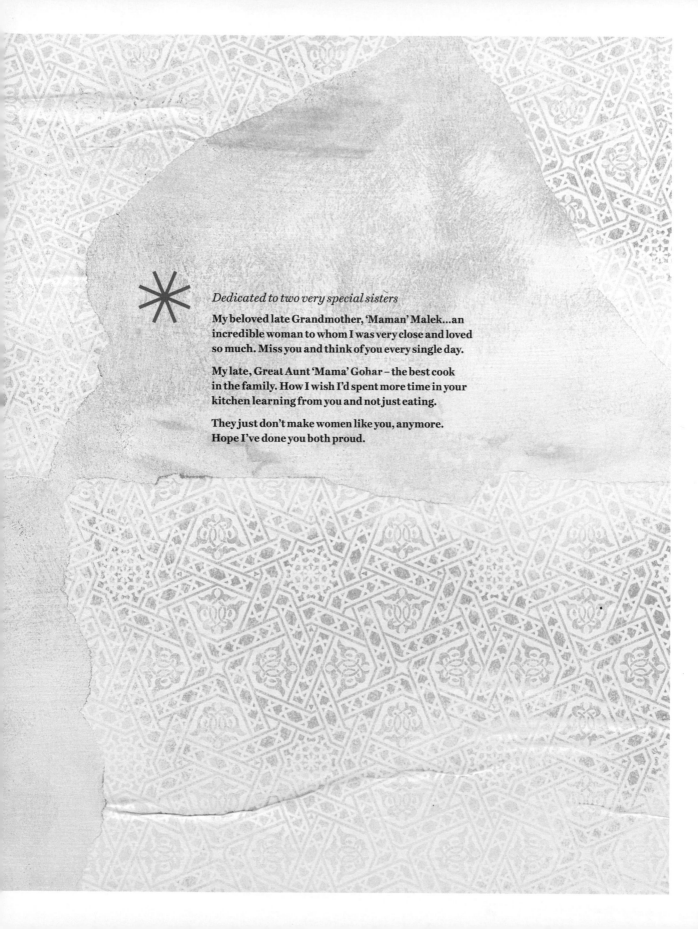

Dedicated to two very special sisters

My beloved late Grandmother, 'Maman' Malek…an incredible woman to whom I was very close and loved so much. Miss you and think of you every single day.

My late, Great Aunt 'Mama' Gohar – the best cook in the family. How I wish I'd spent more time in your kitchen learning from you and not just eating.

They just don't make women like you, anymore. Hope I've done you both proud.

An Hachette UK Company
www.hachette.co.uk

First published in Great Britain in 2016 by Mitchell Beazley,
a division of Octopus Publishing Group Ltd
Carmelite House
50 Victoria Embankment
London EC4Y 0DZ
www.octopusbooks.co.uk

ISBN 978 1 78472 047 6

A CIP catalogue record for this book is available from
the British Library.

Printed and bound in China
10 9 8 7 6 5 4 3 2

CONTENTS

INTRODUCTION

Sirocco noun / si-**roc**-co /

Origin: Early 17th century; from Italian *scirocco*, **based on Spanish Arabic** *sharq* **'east wind'**

A hot, dry wind blowing from east to west – sometimes described as warm, spicy and sultry.

My heritage has given me great insight into understanding the favourite ingredients and flavours of Eastern cuisine, which gives me confidence when using Eastern ingredients. I am never afraid to be bold with my use of spices or flavourings, and I don't hold back when it comes to combining flavours and ingredients. But, in stark contrast to my heritage, I was raised in England and have the advantages of growing up with entirely different produce, ingredients, recipes and cooking techniques to those of my heritage. The result of this culinary cultural blending is that I have gained an understanding of how to combine the beautiful produce I've grown up knowing with Eastern flavours to achieve perfectly balanced flavour combinations that – whether subtle and aromatic or bold and punchy – often improve on the natural flavour of an ingredient.

These recipes are all inspired by flavours of the East but use the fresh produce, techniques and cookery styles of the West; hence the name *Sirocco*. None of these recipes are authentically Middle Eastern – instead, I wanted to share my own style of uncomplicated, full-flavoured recipes that reflect the kind of cooking I do the most.

I learned so much from the comments and wonderful feedback I had from my last book, *Persiana*, which prompted me to continue writing recipes that were straightforward and didn't rely on any particular ingredient to make them successful. I realized that many people feel the pressure to follow recipes to the letter, but Middle Eastern cookery just isn't rigid in that way. In fact, most home-style cookery isn't that way and the best recipes, the ones we keep making time and again, are those in which we can easily substitute an ingredient or two if

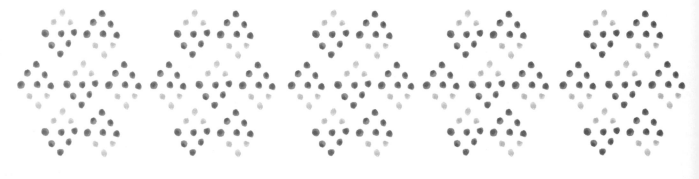

needed, because in today's world, convenience and time are key factors.

Not everything has to be aggressively spiced or full of chilli heat. Sometimes, a wonderful balance and delicate contrast of flavour can deliver a refined subtlety that initially you wouldn't have thought possible. It frustrates me when Middle Eastern food is summed up using the word 'spice' or 'spicy' because this isn't always the case and, often, it is about aromatics, citrus, the fragrance of herbs or even the way in which something is cooked and served. Other times, it can be incredibly simple and pared right down to a key ingredient – an aubergine, simply grilled and served with yogurt, for example. Often, the simplicity of Eastern cuisine is overlooked when, in most cases, the real food of the East is humble, uncomplicated and simple.

I use many of the same spices and store cupboard ingredients from summer into winter. They see me right through the year, from creating the much-needed comfort of wintery, warming stews to the light and refreshing dishes we crave during the warmer months, when fresh produce is green and abundant. *Sirocco* contains bold, vibrant flavour combinations that are great for everyday cooking or for more elaborate get-togethers, in recipes that are still very much steeped in the roots of Middle Eastern cookery, but with a fresher, lighter approach that's more conducive to everyday cooking and enjoyment.

Whether you are looking to prepare several dishes for a family meal or for just a single simple recipe, you can take what you want from this book. If you need a little useful inspiration for breakfast, lunch or dinner, or simply ideas for something to snack on alongside drinks with friends, there is something for everyone. The recipes use accessible ingredients to create unique but familiar dishes that are perfect for any occasion. If you are missing an ingredient, don't stress – just leave it out.

Hopefully, in your kitchen this book will get covered in oil splatter and food stains and remain close to hand (rather than buried under a pile of other books), full of recipes you turn to, time and time again, change and make your own... food that is simply delicious, not Eastern or Western, just straightforward and satisfying.

Sabrina Ghayour

MY KITCHEN STORE CUPBOARD

The contents of your kitchen cupboards say a lot about the kind of cook you are. Mine are so messy and crammed full of every little ingredient possible that I shudder to think what they say about me. There is no order, just chaos: my own kind of comfortable, organized chaos. If there is an inch of unused space, I will find a way of stuffing something into it – but I can live with myself because I always have something in there to transform simple ingredients into something a little more special.

I am the kind of cook who relies on ingredients from the store cupboard to help give a simple dish a little extra flavour. Whether that comes from a single spice or spice mix, a flavoured oil, preserve or unique ingredient, I find great comfort in knowing that I can always combine fresh produce with a little something from the cupboard to make a simple meal more interesting.

The truth of the matter is that we all have tons of ingredients and spices, both familiar and unfamiliar, in our cupboards, often purchased for a single recipe where you use a teaspoon of it, then you are stuck with the rest and don't know what else to do with it. My ethos is very much based on getting the best out of your purchased ingredients – knowing how to use them time and again in different recipes and a myriad of different guises to achieve varied and delicious results every time.

Understanding an individual ingredient and how best to use it is key to ensuring you use up what you've purchased and none goes to waste. I think people can become nervous with an unfamiliar product and use it just the once, and might never learn how to utilize it to its full potential. My recipes are simple and flavourful and that almost all ingredients can be substituted, and most can be left out entirely. Trusting your own instinct, as to what you do and don't like and what you can and can't live without in a dish, is still the secret to becoming a more competent (and confident) cook.

I am often asked what my must-have store cupboard ingredients are, and while some of them are perfectly familiar and well-known items, such as dry spices like cinnamon, cumin, coriander and turmeric, others are lesser known. Here's how to get the best out of them.

✳

Pul Biber Chilli Flakes

A Turkish staple ingredient, these wonderful chilli flakes deliver a gentler chilli kick than the usual red chilli flakes more commonly found. They can be sprinkled on salads or bruschetta, used in pastas, rice dishes and stews and are great on potatoes and root vegetables. Their less aggressive heat means that you can use them more abundantly, yet still taste the core ingredients of a dish – albeit with a pleasing chilli heat.

✳

Za'atar

Essentially a herb mix rather than a spice mix, za'atar is a staple ingredient in much of the Middle East. It is made with wild thyme and toasted sesame seeds. Variations now include sumac, oregano, marjoram and cumin. It is incredibly versatile and can be sprinkled on to salads, sandwiches and cheese or made into a paste with oil and used to marinate meat, poultry, seafood and vegetables. It also bakes beautifully into breads and, with some olive oil, can be used for dipping bread into.

Sumac

A common ingredient in Iran and the Middle East, sumac is a red berry that is dried and ground into a powder for use as a seasoning. Iranians use it very simply to season grilled meats (usually lamb) because the aromatic, citric flavour of the granules cuts through fat beautifully. It's great with fish instead of lemon juice, but especially in salads, on vegetable dishes, mixed with cold butter to make a butter compound, in breads and as part of spice blends for all kinds of meat and poultry. Nowadays I use it in everything.

Pomegranate Molasses

A wonderful staple of any nation that cultivates pomegranates, the molasses (or syrup) is simply a concentrated reduction of raw pomegranate juice. It is sweet with a wickedly sour aftertaste that, when paired with the right ingredients, can be marvellous. I use it as a salad dressing on tomatoes or any mixed-leaf salad, especially when there is a sweet ingredient added to it. It is also a great dressing for grain salads featuring freekeh, brown rice and bulgar wheat and makes a wonderful sauce for game and red meat.

PUL BIBER
CHILLI FLAKES

ZA'ATAR

POMEGRANATE MOLASSES

SUMAC

Harissa

A blend of different chilli peppers and spices, harissa is sold in abundance in markets and is a staple in every home, playing a key role in North African cuisine. I use it in salad dressings, yogurt sauces, mayonnaise, stews, soups, pasta sauces and stir-fries. I fry it with rice and noodles and even mix a little into couscous, bulgar wheat or rice salads to give them some pep. It also makes a great marinade for meat, poultry and chicken destined for the grill, but beware – a little goes a long way.

HARISSA

PRESERVED LEMONS

GREEN VERBENA HARISSA

SAFFRON

WHOLE SPICES

PICKLED CHILLIES

SPICE BLENDS

GARLIC OIL

Preserved Lemons

These wonderful little lemons are packed in salt or brine and preserved to jelly-like perfection. The fact that they are preserved means they have a long life and you can always turn to them when you need to give a dish a little zing. Ready to use in marinades, stews, salads, sandwiches and wraps, and as garnishes and seasonings, they are incredibly useful and give everything an instant perkiness and a sharp-and-salty flavour.

Pickled Chillies

One of my all-time favourite store cupboard ingredients for the sheer convenience factor alone, pickled chillies are used endlessly in my home. Whether in salads, sandwiches, dips, marinades, pastas, rice, noodles, stir-fries and sauces, or served with meat, poultry, fish, vegetables or grilled halloumi, I cannot live without them. They even make the most wonderful addition to a toasted cheese sandwich. They never go off, unlike fresh chillies.

Saffron

Being Iranian, I am fortunate enough to always have access to the best-quality Iranian saffron in abundance. One of my favourite dishes to make is a simple pasta with tinned crab meat, chilli, garlic and saffron, so it's not all Middle Eastern style. Saffron makes mayonnaise, sauces and marinades and gives life and colour to rice dishes, both in the water absorption method (as with paellas and risottos) and in the aromatic steaming method (Persian rice dishes and biryanis). It is also great thrown into tomato sauces and used with seafood and poultry.

Whole Spices

Some of my favourite whole spices are cumin seeds, coriander seeds, green cardamom and black cardamom. Toasting whole spices in a pan and grinding them down into a powder is the best way to get the most out of their flavour.

Spice Blends

Indians call them *masalas*, Lebanese call them *baharat* and Persians say *advieh*. In many homes in the East, a staple and versatile signature spice blend is made and used in various dishes to add flavour and character. The way in which the blend is used can vary greatly and create different dimensions and tastes, despite the same base of spices being used to make the dish. There are some great spice mixes available in supermarkets and Ras El Hanout (a Moroccan spice blend) and baharat (Lebanese) are two of my favourites. I especially love using them to rub or marinate red meats and sweet vegetables such as carrots, butternut squash, sweet potatoes and pumpkin – all of which can hold spice so well.

Garlic Oil

Garlic oil is my secret weapon in the kitchen and I used tonnes of the stuff. A little drizzle can transform a dish, so I use it in everything, from classic roast potatoes and fried mushrooms, meat, poultry and fish to rubs, marinades, dips, dressings and sauces. I even drizzle it over toasted or chargrilled bread when making bruschetta. If you ever run out of garlic or can't be bothered to peel garlic, it is a great substitute.

*

brilliant breakfasts & brunches

STICKY LAMB BUNS
page 92

PEAR, FETA & HONEY TOASTS
page 38

PICKLED CUCUMBER
RELISH *page 92*

BUTTERNUT ROSTIS WITH
POACHED EGGS *page 20*

BACON PITTAS
page 31

BUTTERNUT RÖSTIS
with Poached Eggs

Traditionally made with potatoes, rösti are a great way to use up spare root vegetables or squashes. I like using butternut squash in mine and adding lots of spices to complement the sweet flavour of the squash. These little röstis make a great breakfast or brunch dish, but also work really well as an accompaniment to a main meal, in which case omit the eggs.

SERVES 4

✳

1 small butternut squash, peeled and
    coarsely grated
1 large onion, finely chopped
3 teaspoons sea salt flakes
1 heaped tablespoon plain flour
1 teaspoon turmeric
1 teaspoon ground cumin
1 teaspoon ground coriander

1 teaspoon ground cinnamon
1 bunch of spring onions, thinly sliced
½ small packet (about 15g) of dill, leaves
    and fronds finely chopped
5 large eggs
vegetable oil, for frying
freshly ground black pepper

Put the grated butternut squash and chopped onion in a mixing bowl and add the salt. Using your hands, mix well. The salt will draw out excess moisture from the squash and onion, resulting in crisp rösti. Leave to stand for approximately 30 minutes. Using a sieve or clean cloth, extract as much moisture as you can from the mixture and return it to the mixing bowl.

Preheat the oven to 160°C, Gas Mark 3. Bring a large pan of water to the boil, ready for poaching the eggs. Line a baking tray with baking paper. Heat a large frying pan over a medium heat.

Add the flour, spices, spring onions and dill (reserving 1 teaspoon dill for sprinkling) to the squash and onion mixture and mix well with your hands. Once the spices and dill are evenly incorporated, crack in 1 egg and mix again, adding a generous seasoning of black pepper. Shape the mixture into 12 patties, each approximately 10cm wide and 1cm thick. Heat a good amount of oil in the hot frying pan and fry the patties in batches for 6–8 minutes on one side or until nice and crisp, then flip over and fry on the other side for 5–6 minutes or until deep golden brown. Keep the cooked patties warm in the oven on the prepared baking tray while you fry subsequent batches.

To poach your eggs, stir the boiling water to make a well in the centre and carefully crack the remaining eggs into the water. Cook for 3 minutes (if you like them runny), then remove the eggs from the water with a slotted spoon and plunge them straight into cold water.

Place 3 rösti on each serving plate, top with a poached egg and a little sprinkling of fresh dill and freshly ground black pepper, then serve immediately.

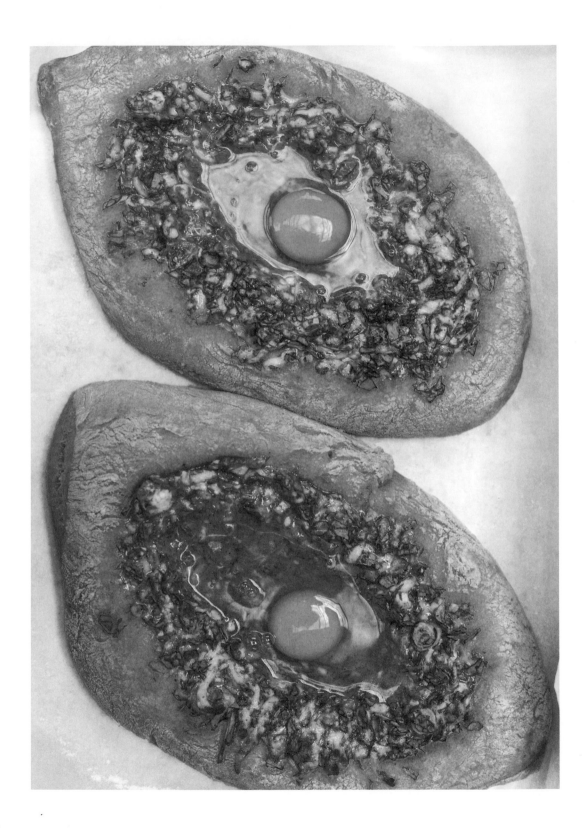

BREAD BOATS

These bread boats are popular in Turkey and Georgia and I can understand why... much like pizza, a bread boat is a complete meal all in one. They are great at any time of day, but I do think they are the perfect brunch dish, and I love this version, with its crowning glory of an egg cracked on top, to finish.

MAKES 4

✳

For the dough

7g sachet fast-action dried yeast

500ml warm water

700g strong white bread flour

2 heaped tablespoons crushed sea salt
flakes

75ml olive oil

For the filling

6 large eggs

250g ready-grated mozzarella (not
Buffalo mozzarella)

120g young spinach leaves, roughly chopped

4 spring onions, thinly sliced

1 teaspoon cayenne pepper

pinch of grated nutmeg

finely grated zest of 1 unwaxed lemon

sea salt flakes and freshly ground
black pepper

Stir the yeast into 50ml of the warm water, then allow it to sit for a few minutes until it has dissolved.

In a large bowl, combine the flour and crushed salt, then make a well in the centre. Pour in the remaining warm water, 50ml of the olive oil and the yeast dissolved in water and combine using your hands until you have a smooth dough. If the dough is a bit too sticky, just add a little extra flour and, if it is dry, an additional splash of warm water.

On a clean, floured surface, knead the dough for 5 minutes to activate the yeast and stretch the glutens within it. Allow the dough to rest for 10 minutes before kneading it again for 2 minutes. Repeat this process another 3 times and, on the second, incorporate the remaining 25ml olive oil. Return the dough to the bowl, cover it with a clean tea towel and leave it to rest for 3 hours. Once the resting period is over, the dough will have tripled in size.

Preheat the oven to 230°C, Gas Mark 8. Line a large baking tray with baking paper. Divide the dough into 4 equal portions and shape each into a 'boat' shape and place on the lined tray. Cover loosely with clingfilm and leave to rest in a warm place for 45–60 minutes.

Make the filling. In a mixing bowl, beat 1 egg with the mozzarella, spinach, spring onions, cayenne, nutmeg and lemon zest and season well with salt and pepper. Blend well until the mixture is smooth.

Divide the mixture into 4 equal portions and place 1 in the centre of each bread boat, leaving 2.5cm clear at the edges. Pick up the clear edges of dough and tuck them inwards to secure the filling. Beat 1 of the remaining eggs and brush any exposed pastry dough with this egg wash. Bake for 15–17 minutes, remove from oven and carefully crack 1 egg into the centre of each boat. Bake for 6–8 minutes more or until the egg whites are opaque.

PARSEE DUCK EGG SCRAMBLE

I can't lie, the first time I was presented with duck eggs I was rather dubious about how they would taste and was worried I wouldn't like them. Now? I am absolutely addicted in a where-have-you-been-all-my-life kind of way. They are so delicious and make the best scrambled eggs you'll ever eat. Their rich and creamy character allows them to hold their own against spices – even better than ordinary hens' eggs do. This is a great breakfast or brunch dish, but in my culture, it's very common to eat eggs for a light but totally fabulous evening meal.

SERVES 4

＊

1 teaspoon cumin seeds

1 teaspoon coriander seeds

vegetable oil, for frying

handful of fresh curry leaves (8 or so)

1 long red chilli, thinly sliced and finely chopped (deseed, if you prefer)

1 fat garlic clove, crushed

½ teaspoon turmeric

1 bunch of spring onions, thinly sliced from root to tip

30g salted butter

6 duck eggs, beaten

zest of 1 unwaxed lime

½ small packet (about 15g) of fresh coriander, finely chopped

sea salt flakes and freshly ground black pepper

Heat a large frying pan over a medium-high heat and toast the cumin and coriander seeds for a few minutes, stirring to prevent burning. Remove the toasted seeds from the pan and grind them to a powder using a pestle and mortar.

Drizzle some oil into the same pan, add the curry leaves and, once they start to make popping noises, add the chilli and garlic, followed by the cumin and coriander powder and the turmeric. Stir well. Add the spring onions and butter, swiftly followed by the beaten duck eggs. Using a wooden spoon, scramble the duck eggs by stirring quickly to prevent sticking. Add a generous seasoning of salt and pepper, the lime zest and fresh coriander, then remove from the heat immediately. Stir and serve, ideally with some warm flatbread or even simple tortilla wraps. I also love chilli sauce or mango chutney with this dish.

AVOCADO MASH ON GRIDDLED SOURDOUGH
with Tahini Dressing

For me, avocado is one of those food-of-the-gods kind of things. I can eat it for breakfast, lunch or dinner and am happy to have it with something, in something or just by itself. So it's a total bonus that avocado is actually good for you! However, I do find that on its own, avocado needs a little help: a pinch of salt, a squeeze of lemon and, as I discovered one day by accident, some tahini dressing – a match made in heaven.

SERVES 2–4

✳

2 large ripe avocados

2 tablespoons garlic oil

3 spring onions, thinly sliced from root to tip

1 long red chilli, deseeded and finely chopped

½ small packet (about 15g) of fresh coriander, finely chopped

1 teaspoon ground coriander

4 slices of sourdough or bread of your choice

extra virgin olive oil, for drizzling

sea salt flakes and freshly ground black pepper

For the tahini dressing

2 heaped teaspoons tahini

2 teaspoons Greek-style yogurt

finely grated zest and juice of 1 large unwaxed lemon

2 tablespoons cold water

Preheat a griddle pan over a high heat.

Scoop out the avocado flesh into a bowl, add the garlic oil and a generous amount of salt and pepper and lightly mash the avocado with a fork. Switch to a spoon, add the spring onions, chilli, fresh coriander and ground coriander and mix well. Set aside.

Brush the sourdough bread with olive oil on both sides and chargrill on the hot griddle pan for 2 minutes on each side or until char marks appear on each side.

In a small bowl, combine the tahini, yogurt, lemon zest and juice and the 2 tablespoons of water together until an even sauce is formed and the tahini is fully dissolved. Season well with salt.

To serve, divide the avocado mixture into 4 portions and spoon 1 portion over each slice of toast. Drizzle over the tahini sauce to finish and add an extra glug of olive oil, if you wish.

BUTTERNUT, SAGE & TULUM PAN TOASTIES

Sometimes, you just need a really quick meal. The Italians have pizza, the Mexicans have quesadillas and I make pan toasties. Why pan toasties? Well, there was a rather long period when I didn't own a toaster, so I became pretty nifty at making a variety of toasted sandwiches using a dry frying pan. I've used everything from regular white bread and focaccia to khobz and lavash, but the bread that stood out (perhaps purely because it was frying pan sized and shaped) was the humble flour tortilla. Tulum is a wonderful salty Turkish cheese traditionally made in animal hides, but if you can't find it then feta or a strong sharp cheese will work well, too.

MAKES 2

✳

½ small butternut squash (unpeeled), quartered and deseeded
olive oil, for drizzling
5 sage leaves, finely chopped, or 1 heaped tablespoon dried sage
2 flour tortillas
150g tulum cheese (or use feta cheese or grated mozzarella cheese)
1 teaspoon pul biber chilli flakes (optional)
sea salt flakes and freshly ground black pepper

Preheat the oven to 200°C, Gas Mark 6. Line a baking tray with baking paper.

Place the butternut squash on the prepared baking tray, drizzle with olive oil and season with a generous amount of salt and pepper. Roast the squash for 40 minutes until soft. Set aside until cool enough to handle, then scoop out flesh into a bowl and fork through it gently, adding the sage and a good amount of salt and pepper to taste.

Place a large frying pan over a medium heat and allow the pan to heat up. Put 1 tortilla into the pan, then crumble half the tulum cheese all over the tortilla. Divide the butternut mixture into 2 equal portions and gently cover half the tortilla with 1 portion of the butternut mixture and, if you like it spicy and want to add the pul biber, sprinkle half of it over the filling. Fold the clear half of the tortilla over the butternut mixture and pat it down to make a semicircle. Toast on both sides until golden brown. Repeat with the remaining ingredients. Serve immediately.

TWO-CHEESE MELTS
with Thyme-roasted Onions

Everything about this recipe reminds me of my cousin Cyrus. He is the most chaotic and experimental cook I know, but his food is always wonderful. I'm very impressed by his bravery – he is an empty-the-contents-of-your-fridge-and-cupboard-and-see-what-happens kind of cook, yet his concoctions always hit the spot. Cyrus was a guinea pig for several of the recipes that appeared in *Persiana*, and he is very much my inspiration for this recipe.

SERVES 2

✳

2 red onions

olive oil, for drizzling

2 teaspoons dried thyme

2 large slices of thick, good-quality bread (I like to use sourdough)

100g mature or extra mature Cheddar cheese, grated

100g feta cheese, crumbled

½ teaspoon cayenne pepper

freshly ground black pepper

Preheat the oven to 240°C, Gas Mark 9. Line a baking tray with baking paper.

Halve the red onions from root to tip, then cut each half into 3 segments. Place these on the prepared baking tray and drizzle with olive oil. Use your hands to toss the onion wedges in oil. Sprinkle with the thyme. Roast for 18 minutes or until the onions are cooked and browned around edges.

Toast the bread to your liking. Place the grated Cheddar and crumbled feta cheese in a small saucepan along with the cayenne pepper and a good amount of black pepper and begin to melt them slowly over a gentle heat, stirring regularly to ensure the cheese is melting. Once the cheese has melted, take the pan off the heat and stir the mixture again.

Pour half of the melted cheese mixture over each slice of toast and serve at room temperature with the roasted onions.

BACON PITTAS

Nothing beats a great bacon sarnie for breakfast... or so I thought until I was served a bacon naan in Dishoom restaurant in London. Their bacon naans, generously stuffed with chunky, crispy bacon and a spicy-sweet sauce, are absolutely epic. This is my humble homage to the great bacon naan of Dishoom – a wonderful bacon sandwich at any time of day.

SERVES 4

✳

For the pitta

5g fast-action dried yeast

150ml warm water

250g plain flour

1 heaped teaspoon fine sea salt

2 tablespoons garlic oil

For the filling

6 tablespoons mango chutney

4 tablespoons ketchup

1 long red chilli, deseeded and finely chopped

1 teaspoon ground cinnamon

1 teaspoon ground cumin

12–16 slices of smoked or unsmoked streaky bacon

4 spring onions, thinly sliced

½ small packet (about 15g) of fresh coriander, roughly chopped

First, make the pitta. Dissolve the yeast in the 150ml of warm water and leave the mixture to sit for 5 minutes. Combine the flour, salt and garlic oil in a mixing bowl, then pour in the dissolved yeast and blend to form a dough. Knead the dough for a couple of minutes, then cover with a clean tea towel and leave somewhere warm and dry to rest for 1 hour.

Meanwhile, make the filling. Put the mango chutney, ketchup, chilli, cinnamon and cumin in a small saucepan set over a medium heat and bring the mixture to a gentle simmer, stirring to avoid burning. Take the pan off the heat and set aside.

Preheat the oven to 140°C, Gas Mark 1.

Grill or fry the bacon according to your preference. I like to fry mine in a preheated large frying pan with a little oil, crisping up the slices nicely on both sides for a couple of minutes. Remove the bacon from the pan, drain, cover it with kitchen foil and keep it warm in the preheated oven while you finish making the flatbread.

After the proving time has elapsed, heat a large, heavy-based frying pan over a high heat. Divide the mixture into 4 dough balls and roll them out to 5mm-thick rounds. Allow them to rest for 5–6 minutes, then place them directly on the dry pan and cook until the edges begin to come away from the pan (about 45 seconds). Flip them over and cook on the other side for 30–45 seconds. Place the cooked flatbreads on a clean tea towel while you finish cooking the remaining dough rounds.

To serve, split open each pitta and put 3–4 slices of bacon inside it. Drizzle in some of the sauce and sprinkle with spring onions and coriander. Serve immediately.

CARDAMOM DOUGHNUT BRIOCHE FRENCH TOASTS

Doughnuts are a weakness of mine. Mind you, not just any old doughnut will do… I like mine without any filling, rolled in sugar, and no strong flavours. For me, simple is always best. This dish was inspired by domestic goddess Nigella Lawson's doughnut French toast recipe from her book *Nigella Express*, which became a family favourite. While I love ordinary French toast, I tend to alternate between cinnamon and cardamom flavours for this recipe, so if you want to go with the cinnamon version, omit the cardamom and add 2 heaped teaspoons of cinnamon to the caster sugar instead.

SERVES 2

✳

100g caster sugar

seeds from 4 green cardamom pods, ground using a pestle and mortar

2 eggs

2 tablespoons milk

zest of 1 unwaxed orange

1 teaspoon vanilla bean paste (or use vanilla extract)

4 slices of brioche, each 2.5cm thick

50g butter

Heat a large frying pan over a medium heat. Combine the sugar and cardamom powder in a bowl until evenly blended. Pour the mixture on to a flat plate and smooth it out.

Put the eggs, milk, orange zest and vanilla bean paste in a bowl and beat until evenly combined. Pour into a shallow dish with a flat base and soak 2 slices of brioche in the mixture for about 45 seconds before flipping them over and soaking for another 45 seconds. Meanwhile, melt half the butter in the warm pan. Fry the 2 soaked slices of brioche for 2 minutes on each side until puffed up (which indicates that the egg is cooked) and golden brown. Immediately place the cooked brioche slices in the cardamom sugar, coating it well on both sides, then transfer to a plate. Repeat with the remaining 2 slices of brioche. Serve immediately.

SOUR CHERRY & RICOTTA PANCAKES
with Clotted Cream & Honey

When I think of pancakes, I think of lazy Sunday mornings when – ideally – someone else is making pancakes for me. I love nuts, chocolate chips and lots of different fruits in my pancakes, but nothing is more Persian than adding sour cherries. I like to use the sweetened ones as, otherwise, they can be quite sour. Instead of butter or maple syrup, I prefer clotted cream and honey – heavenly – and just the kind of indulgence needed for a weekend of pure laziness and enjoyment.

MAKES 16–18 PANCAKES

*

100g dried and sweetened sour cherries (or use cranberries), roughly chopped

6 tablespoons water

2 tablespoons caster sugar

few knobs of butter

1 large egg

150g self-raising flour

250ml milk

generous pinch of sea salt flakes, crushed

250g ricotta

clear honey, to drizzle

clotted cream, to serve

Heat a small saucepan over a medium heat. Put the sour cherries into the pan along with the 6 tablespoons of water, the sugar and a knob of butter. Gently heat the mixture as the cherries hydrate. After 5–6 minutes take the pan off the heat and leave the mixture to cool.

Heat a large frying pan over a medium-high heat.

In a mixing bowl, combine the egg, flour, milk and crushed salt and whisk well without over-beating the mixture. Don't worry if the batter is not perfectly smooth. Stir in the ricotta.

Put a couple of knobs of butter into the hot pan and pour in a generous tablespoon of the batter to make 1 pancake. Cook as many pancakes as you can simultaneously without overcrowding the pan. After cooking for roughly 1 minute, flip over the pancakes and cook for 1 minute on the other side or until golden brown. Repeat until all the batter has been used.

Serve the pancakes with a good drizzle of clear honey, a few dollops of clotted cream and the cherries.

PEAR, FETA
& HONEY TOASTS

I have a thing for feta drizzled with honey. I have tried to find the roots of my bizarre addiction, and no other Iranians seem to like that combination. Both my Greek and Turkish friends thought that my craving was weird (until they became converts, after trying it) and people still seem a bit put off by the pairing. I promise you, it is an addictive thing if you like sweet and savoury combinations. This dish is great for breakfast and brunch, but – truthfully – it's lovely to snack on at any time of day. The addition of pear gives it a juicy burst of flavour.

SERVES 2–4

*

1 large, ripe pear (I like to use red pears)
4 slices of good-quality bread of your choice, each 2.5cm thick
200g feta cheese
2 tablespoons clear honey
freshly ground black pepper

Quarter the pear lengthways and remove the stalk, core and seeds. Cut the quarters into thin slices and set aside.

Toast the bread slices and, once toasted, divide the feta into 4 portions. Crumble 1 portion on to each slice of toast, and arrange the pear slices in an overlapping fan-like pattern on top. Drizzle each slice with ½ tablespoon honey, season with freshly ground black pepper and serve.

ROSE & SPICE INFUSED BERRIES
with Citrus Honey Yogurt

While many people start the day with yogurt, I can say with my hand on my heart that I never have. I enjoy toast in the mornings, but I do like having yogurt with brunch or as an afternoon snack, for which this dish is ideal. It would also make a great dessert as it has lots of flavour, but is a lighter way to end a meal if you are planning a feast. You can either plate it up individually or serve it all on a large platter for sharing.

SERVES 4

✳

50g caster sugar

200ml cold water

4 tablespoons rose water

1 teaspoon ground cinnamon

4 green cardamom pods, lightly crushed

pinch of nutmeg

2 tablespoons dried edible rose petals, finely chopped

zest of 1 unwaxed orange

zest of 1 unwaxed lime

4 tablespoons clear honey

300g thick Greek yogurt

200g blackberries, chilled

200g blueberries, chilled

200g strawberries, chilled

200g raspberries, chilled

handful of mint leaves, finely chopped

Heat a small saucepan over a medium-low heat. Add the sugar, the 200ml of water, the rose water, cinnamon, cardamom pods, nutmeg and rose petals (reserving 1 teaspoon petals for garnishing) to the pan and heat gently for approximately 10 minutes until the sugar dissolves and the mixture thickens just a touch. Take the pan off the heat and leave the mixture to cool to room temperature.

In a mixing bowl, mix the orange and lime zest, honey and Greek yogurt until evenly combined. Refrigerate the mixture until ready to serve.

Once the syrup has cooled to room temperature, put the berries into a bowl and pour over the syrup. Using a metal spoon, coat the berries in the syrup, working carefully to ensure you don't crush them. Cover the bowl with clingfilm and refrigerate for 1 hour.

About 30 minutes before serving, remove the berries from the refrigerator to bring them up to room temperature. Stir the chopped mint carefully through the berry mixture, then, using a slotted spoon, serve the berries on top of the yogurt. Using a teaspoon, drizzle a generous amount of the syrup over and serve with a sprinkling of the reserved chopped rose petals.

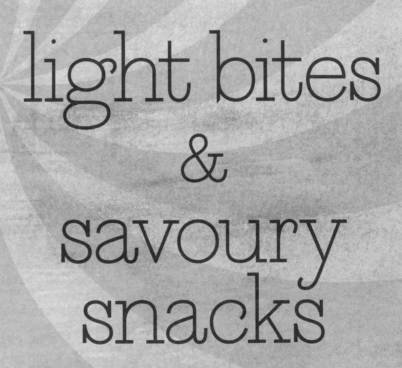

*

light bites
&
savoury
snacks

VINE-BAKED FETA
page 80

ORANGE, THYME & SPICE
CHICKEN WINGS *page 96*

CHARGRILLED
COURGETTES *page 62*

APPLE, SUMAC, RED ONION &
POMEGRANATE SALAD *page 110*

CHICKENBERRY RICE
page 170

TAMARIND HONEY PRAWNS
page 104

SWEET SPICE-ROASTED NUTS

We produce a huge variety of nuts in Iran and I really love snacking on them – although I find myself eating way too many at times. We don't roast them with seasonings as is done in the West, but I do like spicy, sticky coatings on any kind of nut. These spicy nuts are great as a snack, added to salads and even chopped up and sprinkled over desserts.

SERVES 6

✳

500g unroasted nuts (I used 150g macadamia, 250g cashew nuts and 100g almonds)

4 tablespoons melted butter

4 tablespoons soft brown sugar

good squeeze of lemon juice

2 tablespoons pul biber chilli flakes

2 teaspoons ground cinnamon

1 teaspoon ground coriander

sea salt flakes

Preheat the oven to 170°C, Gas Mark 3½. Line a baking tray with baking paper. Place the nuts on the prepared tray and toast for 10 minutes.

Put the melted butter in a bowl, add the sugar, lemon juice, spices and a generous seasoning of salt and mix well. Add the toasted nuts. Coat the nuts well in the mixture, stirring to break up any clumps of sugar or spice. Once they are evenly coated, place the nuts back on the baking tray and toast for another 5 minutes. Using a spoon, turn the nuts, then return them to the oven for a further 5 minutes.

Allow to cool slightly before serving. Once fully cooled, they can be stored in a glass preserving jar or another airtight container in a cool, dry place, but should be consumed within a few days.

I like to serve these with Hibiscus Coolers (see page 49) and Dried Broad Bean & Cashew Nut Dip and flatbread (see page 48).

DRIED BROAD BEAN & CASHEW NUT DIP

This wonderful dip (see photograph on page 47) has taken over from hummus in my house. Dried broad beans are underrated in Western culture. So many people who have tasted this dip have told me they didn't even know you could find dried broad beans. You can, although you may need to hunt around a little. But when you find them, stock up, as they store well and have many uses. I invented this recipe by accident. One day, with only one packet of broad beans left, I opened my cupboard in search of something to bulk up a dip and, lo and behold, there were some cashew nuts. I toasted them and added them to the mix and the result was even better than its previous incarnation – which is why I have to share this recipe with you.

SERVES 6

✳

200g dried broad beans

200g toasted cashew nuts

1 teaspoon thyme leaves, finely chopped, plus extra to garnish

2 garlic cloves, peeled and crushed

finely grated zest and juice of 2 large lemons

4 tablespoons garlic oil

4–6 tablespoons olive oil, plus extra for drizzling

sea salt flakes and freshly ground black pepper

Boil the dried broad beans according to the packet instructions until cooked and soft (approximately 45 minutes, depending on the size of the beans used). Drain and set aside, reserving some of the boiling liquid in case you need it to slacken the mixture later.

Put the drained broad beans, the cashew nuts, thyme, crushed garlic, lemon zest and juice, garlic oil, olive oil and a generous quantity of salt and pepper into a food processor and blitz until broken down. If the mixture is too thick, add a little of the reserved liquid (or more olive oil, if preferred) and blitz again until smooth. Taste the mixture and adjust the seasoning if necessary (the dip does like a lot of salt, as broad beans are naturally sweet).

Transfer the dip to a bowl. Sprinkle over the remaining thyme leaves, drizzle with a little olive oil and serve.

HIBISCUS COOLER

Hibiscus, when dried or preserved, can be used in myriad ways in cakes and desserts, sweets, marinades and drinks. A version of this drink is enjoyed everywhere from Egypt to Jamaica, but my version is a delicious hibiscus-infused lemon drink (see photograph on page 47). To make it more grown up, spike it with rum or vodka to make a punch.

MAKES APPROXIMATELY 2 LITRES

✳

50g dried hibiscus flowers

400ml boiling water

1.5 litres chilled water

juice of 4 lemons

200–300g caster sugar

ice cubes, to serve

Put the flowers in a large jug, add the boiling water and leave to infuse for 30 minutes.

Add the chilled water and the lemon juice, then stir in the caster sugar and sweeten to taste. Strain and chill, then serve in tumblers over ice cubes.

PAN-FRIED FIGS

in Serrano Ham

I absolutely love the sweetness of figs, especially when added to savoury dishes. They seem to be a natural partner for anything salty, such as cheese, but also for cured meats such as prosciutto and my favourite, Spanish Jamón – a cured salty ham. These little snacks make ideal finger food, but are also a great addition to a salad, and they take next to no time to put together.

MAKES 16

✳

2 tablespoons olive oil, plus extra for frying

finely grated zest of 1 lemon

freshly ground black pepper

4 large figs (ideally black), quartered

1 heaped tablespoon za'atar

8 slices of Serrano ham (or Prosciutto), halved lengthways into long strips

best-quality aged balsamic vinegar

Drizzle the olive oil into a bowl and mix in the lemon zest and a very generous amount of black pepper. Rub a little of the flavoured oil on to the cut sides of each fig quarter. Then sprinkle a little za'atar on to each quarter. Now wrap a strip of Serrano ham around each fig piece, overlapping the edges of the ham so that most of the fig piece is covered by ham. Repeat until all the pieces are used.

Heat a large frying pan over a high heat. Once it is hot, drizzle in a little olive oil and fry the figs on both cut sides for 1 minute or so until the ham crisps up and browns a little. Once cooked, drizzle with some syrupy well-aged balsamic vinegar and serve immediately.

SUPPER CLUB SPECIAL

Simply put, this is my go-to cocktail for every event. I served it for four years straight at my supper clubs and countless events because it is so easy to make for large groups – just what you need when you are doing all the cooking for a room full of hungry guests!

SERVES 2

✳

2 sprigs of fresh mint

ice cubes or crushed ice

100ml vodka

200ml cloudy apple juice

Drop a mint sprig in each glass and add some ice. Pour 50ml vodka into each glass and top up with apple juice. Stir, then serve.

BUTTER BEAN & ZA'ATAR DIP

This dip is one of those lifesavers that can be put together using mostly staples from your store cupboard when you have surprise guests. Great with crudités, too.

SERVES 4–6

✳

400g can butter beans, drained

2 tablespoons za'atar

3 tablespoons garlic oil

1 tablespoon olive oil, plus extra
 for drizzling

juice of ½ large lemon

2 generous pinches of sea salt flakes

4 tablespoons Greek yogurt

Place all the ingredients in a mixing bowl and, using a hand-held blender, blitz together until you have a smooth, evenly blended mixture. (Alternatively, you can blend the ingredients together in a food processor.) Decant into a serving dish and drizzle with a little extra olive oil and sprinkle with extra za'atar if you like. Serve with toasted pittas, crudités, crisp bread or crisps.

PRESERVED LEMON MARTINI

Being obsessed with the salty-sharp flavour of preserved lemons, I came up with this perfectly balanced Vodka Martini (see photograph on page 50) – it is so smooth and drinkable that you may only realize you've had one too many when it's a little too late!

SERVES 2–4

✳

6 preserved lemons, deseeded and roughly chopped

3 tablespoons water

2 tablespoons clear honey

180ml vodka

ice, to shake

4 preserved lemon slices, to garnish

Put the chopped preserved lemons into a saucepan with the 3 tablespoons of water and bring to the boil, then remove from the heat and leave to cool.

Pour the preserved lemons into a mixing bowl, then blitz with a hand-held blender. Stir in the honey, then add the vodka and mix well.

Fill a cocktail shaker with ice and add the mixture. Shake for 3 minutes, then strain into chilled martini glasses and garnish each with a slice of preserved lemon.

AFGHANI-STYLE SMOKED AUBERGINE DIP

Every nation in the Middle East embraces aubergine in one form or another. I often call it the meat of the Middle East although it's a vegetable, of course. This delicious dish was made for me by my Aunt Azita, whose husband is Afghani. It is great as part of a feast but, quite frankly, it is also really good on its own with some toasted pitta bread.

SERVES 6

✳

4 large aubergines

1 tablespoon cumin seeds, toasted and finely ground

1 teaspoon cayenne pepper

2–3 garlic cloves, crushed

2 tablespoons olive oil, plus extra for drizzling

finely grated zest of 1 lemon and juice of ½

200g thick Greek yogurt

½ small packet (about 15g) of fresh coriander, leaves finely chopped

sea salt flakes and freshly ground black pepper

Blister the aubergines, either by placing them directly on the flame of a gas hob or on a barbecue. Blacken and char the skins all around the aubergines by turning them over from time to time, until the skins are burnt and you can feel that the flesh within them has collapsed. Once done, place the aubergines on a heatproof surface or tray and set aside until cool enough to handle.

Cut the aubergines to open them. Using a large metal spoon, scoop out the pulp, drain off all the excess liquid from it and place it in a bowl (discard the skins). Add the ground cumin, cayenne pepper and garlic and mix well with a fork to break down the pulp. Then add the olive oil, lemon zest and juice, yogurt, fresh coriander and a generous quantity of salt and pepper and mix well. Once combined, taste and adjust the seasoning if necessary, then drizzle with olive oil and serve.

SPICED BEETROOT YOGURT

I do love a dish that comes together quickly yet delivers on flavour, and this is one such dish. I always keep vacuum-packed beetroot in the refrigerator as it has a long shelf life, and since I always keep feta to hand too, it means I can always create a quick and easy meal. Persians love beetroot, especially in yogurt, so I came up with this gently spiced version that is wonderfully refreshing. The sweetness of the beetroot works beautifully with the creamy sharpness of the yogurt. The colour of this dish is quite impressive too – after all, we do eat with our eyes as well as our mouths. If your dip looks a bit pale, simply blend in a couple of extra beetroot to brighten the colour.

SERVES 6

✳

500g cooked beetroot (not in vinegar)

3 tablespoons ground coriander

20g mint, leaves finely chopped

500g Greek yogurt

1 teaspoon nigella seeds

olive oil, for drizzling

sea salt flakes and freshly ground black pepper

Drain the excess juice from the beetroot and blitz them in a bowl using a hand-held blender until they are broken down to a coarse-textured purée. Add the ground coriander, a generous seasoning of salt and pepper and the chopped mint (reserving a generous pinch of mint for garnish) and mix well. Now stir in the Greek yogurt until it is evenly incorporated.

Taste and adjust the seasoning if necessary. Serve with a sprinkling of nigella seeds, the reserved chopped mint and a drizzle of olive oil.

BROCCOLI, BARBERRY & CHILLI FRITTERS

I may have been one of the only children who wasn't force-fed broccoli as a kid, and therefore I absolutely love the stuff. Cooked or raw, to me it is absolutely delicious so I am constantly thinking up new ways to use it. Here is one such idea, which is not only very simple to prepare, but also makes for a delicious end result.

SERVES 4

✳

vegetable oil, approximately 500ml, for frying

300g broccoli florets (include the stalks if you have them)

2 long red chillies, deseeded and very finely chopped

4 spring onions, thinly sliced from root to tip

finely grated zest of 2 unwaxed lemons

3 tablespoons barberries, roughly chopped

4 tablespoons plain flour

1 teaspoon baking powder

4 large eggs

sea salt flakes and freshly ground black pepper

Heat a large, deep frying pan or a large saucepan over a medium-high heat, pour in the oil and allow it to heat up.

Meanwhile, in a small food processor, blitz the broccoli until coarsely chopped. Transfer to a bowl. Add the chillies, spring onions, lemon zest, barberries, flour, baking powder and eggs and mix well until you have a thick batter. Season well with salt and pepper and set aside.

Spoon 1 tablespoon of the mixture into the oil to test how hot the oil is – if the batter sizzles immediately, your oil is hot enough. You will need to fry the fritters in batches to avoid overcrowding the pan. Add tablespoonfuls of the batter to the oil and fry for a few minutes, turning the fritters after 1 minute or so to ensure they are a deep golden brown on both sides. Using a slotted metal spoon, remove the fritters and drain on a plate lined with kitchen paper. Fry the remaining batter in the same way, then serve immediately.

COURGETTE FRIES

with Sumac Salt

I have the Italians to thank for my love of *zucchine fritte*. Crispy lengths of battered courgettes always remind me of holidays in beautiful Italy. Nothing could be simpler to make, but the level of satisfaction I get from eating them is utterly unrivalled. The truth is I can eat mountains of them because they feel lighter than potatoes, which, of course they are… although perhaps not in the volume I like to consume them.

SERVES 6

✳

750ml milk

750g courgettes, cut into 5mm-thick batons (or cut them any way you like)

2 tablespoons sumac

1 tablespoon sea salt flakes

vegetable oil (approximately 1 litre), for frying

300g plain flour

Pour the milk into a shallow bowl, add the courgette batons and leave to soak for 1 hour.

Using a pestle and mortar, grind the sumac with the salt until evenly combined. Set aside.

Heat a large saucepan over a high heat, pour in the oil and heat it up, ready for frying.

Put the flour into a large baking tray with sides that are 5–7cm tall, then shake the pan gently to evenly coat. Drain the courgettes in a colander and shake off any excess moisture. Add them to the flour and dredge them in it, using your hands to coat them lightly without allowing the flour to cake. Remove them with a slotted spoon, shaking off any excess flour, then transfer to a plate and set aside.

Line some plates with kitchen paper. To check that the temperature of the oil is hot enough for frying, add 1 piece of courgette – if it sizzles a lot immediately, the oil is ready. Cooking in batches (depending on the size of your pan), fry the courgettes until each piece is golden brown and crispy, then remove from the pan using a slotted spoon and drain on the paper-lined plates. Serve with a generous seasoning of the prepared sumac salt.

CHARGRILLED COURGETTES
with Goats' Cheese & Sumac

These little beauties make for an impressive starter or side dish and are absolutely delicious. Chargrilling vegetables is such a lovely way to cook them – it avoids overcooking and the charring itself imparts a wonderful flavour. If you don't fancy courgettes, try making rolls with thinly sliced aubergines. Both work well and make a great addition to a feast with friends.

MAKES 10–12 CANAPÉS

✳

3 large courgettes

olive oil, for brushing

200g goats' cheese

3 heaped teaspoons sumac

finely grated zest of 2 unwaxed lemons

good handful of basil leaves, finely chopped

50g toasted pine nuts, roughly chopped

freshly ground black pepper

Preheat a griddle pan over a high heat.

Cut away the stalk and base of the courgette and discard. Using a very sharp knife, cut the courgettes lengthways as straight as you can into 5mm-thick strips (discard the first and last slices of outer skin). Brush 1 side of the courgette strips with olive oil and chargrill for 3 minutes. Brush the uppersides with oil, turn over the strips and chargrill for 3 minutes on the other side until the strips are cooked through and have nice char marks on both sides. If they are not cooked all the way through, they will break when you roll them, so cook for a little longer if necessary. Repeat until all the strips are chargrilled, remove them from the griddle pan and place on a heatproof tray. Leave to cool, then refrigerate for 1 hour.

Meanwhile, make the filling. Crumble the goats' cheese into a bowl, add the sumac, a generous milling of black pepper and the lemon zest and mash them together using a fork until the mixture is evenly blended. Add the basil and pine nuts and blend again until the new additions have been evenly incorporated into the mixture. Refrigerate until the chilling time for the courgettes has elapsed.

Place the courgette strips on a clean surface. Divide the filling mixture into enough equal portions to fill the number of courgette strips you have. Place 1 portion of the filling on to each strip and carefully spread it along three-quarters of the length of the strip. Now roll up the strip in a tight coil, working towards the filling-free edge. Repeat with the remaining strips and portions of filling. Don't worry if the strips break as you roll – the filling will act as a glue of sorts, holding the rolls together. Insert a cocktail stick into each roll at the end of the courgette strip. Refrigerate the rolls for 20 minutes, then serve.

FRIED SEMOLINA-CRUSTED AUBERGINES WITH HONEY

I had a similar version of this dish at Lolita, one of my favourite taperias in Barcelona. They fried slices of semolina-coated aubergines, then drizzled sugar cane molasses over them and that was it. I fell for it hook, line and sinker. This is my slightly adjusted version, substituting honey for the molasses because it is readily available and produces just as delicious a result as the real deal.

SERVES 4–6

✳

3 large aubergines
vegetable oil, for frying
200ml milk
6 tablespoons semolina
sea salt flakes, crushed
75ml clear honey
pul biber chilli flakes, to serve (optional)

Peel the aubergines and cut them into 3.5cm-thick discs. Then cut each slice roughly into pieces about 5cm or so in diameter. Shape variation doesn't matter and neither does size inconsistency – just make the pieces roughly around the same size so that they cook at the same pace.

Pour about 5cm vegetable oil into a large, deep frying pan or wok (or a saucepan, if like me, you prefer to contain oil splatter) and heat the oil over a high heat until hot.

Pour the milk into a small bowl. Tip the semolina on to a small side plate and season it well with crushed salt. Dip the aubergine pieces into the milk, then shake off any excess milk and immediately roll the pieces in the seasoned semolina. Cooking in batches, put the coated aubergine pieces into the hot oil and fry for approximately 1 minute, then turn the pieces to fry the other sides until both sides are nice and brown and the flesh is cooked through in the centre. Drain on to a tray or plate lined with kitchen paper to soak up excess oil. Repeat with subsequent batches. Serve with a good drizzle of clear honey and a sprinkling of pul biber chilli flakes, if liked.

STUFFED BABY AUBERGINES
with Tahini & Garlic

Recipes are often described as 'de-constructed'. Well, this one is a 're-constructed' version of Baba Ghanoush. Traditionally made with smoked aubergine pulp, I keep the aubergines intact and simply roast these babies in an oven tray instead (I always give things my own little twist). I think whole baby aubergines are pleasing to the eye and they have as much flavour as full-sized aubergines – just in a smaller package.

MAKES 16 HALVES

✴

8 baby aubergines, preferably 10–12cm long (not including the stalk)
olive oil, for brushing
2–3 teaspoons tahini
½ small packet (about 15g) of fresh coriander, finely chopped
2 garlic cloves, crushed
finely grated zest of 1 unwaxed lemon and juice of ½
sea salt flakes and freshly ground black pepper

To garnish
1 heaped teaspoon toasted sesame seeds
chopped coriander

Preheat the oven to 200°C, Gas Mark 6. Line a large baking tray with baking paper.

Leaving the stalks intact, slice the aubergines in half lengthways and lay them on the prepared baking tray. Using a pastry brush (or use your fingers) brush olive oil all over the aubergine halves. Roast for 25–30 minutes. Remove from the oven and set aside until cool enough to handle.

Using a teaspoon, carefully scoop out as much flesh as you can from each aubergine half without breaking the skin. Place the pulp into a small bowl and combine it with the tahini, coriander, crushed garlic and lemon zest and juice, and season with salt and pepper.

Increase the oven temperature to 220°C, Gas Mark 7. Carefully spoon the mixture into the aubergine skins, compressing the filling gently to prevent it collapsing during cooking. Place the filled aubergine skins on the oven tray and roast for 12 minutes or until golden brown on top. Serve warm, sprinkled with toasted sesame seeds and chopped coriander.

SPINACH & WALNUT BALLS

I first came across this dish in a Georgian restaurant in Budapest, of all places. It's not the sort of thing I would normally go for on a menu but I was surprised at how good it was. These balls can be prepared in any size and are great as part of a feast or as finger food, served with a thick yogurt. The mixture that's used to make the balls is such a delicious concoction, it also works very well when loosened with yogurt to make a dip for pitta bread or crudités, and I have included this variation below.

SERVES 10 AS A SIDE DISH

✳

750g young spinach leaves

300g walnut halves

4 baby leeks, washed and finely chopped

2 fat garlic cloves, crushed

2 tablespoons dried fenugreek leaves

1 teaspoon cayenne pepper

1 onion, finely chopped

50g flat leaf parsley, leaves finely chopped

50g fresh coriander, finely chopped

3 tablespoons white wine vinegar

olive oil

sea salt flakes and freshly ground black pepper

100g pomegranate seeds, to garnish

If making into a dip

500g thick Greek-style yogurt

Bring a large pan of water to the boil over a high heat and blanch the spinach for approximately 2 minutes, ensuring the blanched leaves retain their vibrant green colour. Remove the spinach from the hot water and plunge the leaves into a bowl of ice-cold water. Leave for a few minutes to allow the spinach to cool down, then drain the leaves, squeeze off any excess moisture and finely chop. Set aside.

In a food processor, blitz the walnuts, leeks, garlic, fenugreek and cayenne pepper together until finely ground. Transfer the mixture to a large mixing bowl. Now blitz the onion until finely chopped but not so much that water leaches out. Add the onion to the mixing bowl along with the chopped spinach and mix well. Add in the fresh parsley and coriander before mixing well. Season generously with salt and pepper to taste and add the vinegar and just enough olive oil to slacken the mixture. Cover and refrigerate for 30–60 minutes.

To make into balls, remove the mixture from the refrigerator, drain off any excess liquid and shape the mixture into balls, or into flattened patty shapes, if you prefer. Garnish generously with the pomegranate seeds and serve.

To make a dip, make the mixture as above, then after chilling remove the mixture from the refrigerator and stir in the yogurt. Check and adjust the seasoning, if necessary, then serve.

COURGETTE, SAFFRON & POTATO KUKU

In Persian, 'kuku' simply refers to an egg-based, frittata-type dish, and I shared the classic recipe, using herbs and barberries, in my book *Persiana*. This is a slightly different take on another version that uses potatoes – but with added courgette and saffron for extra flavour. Kuku is brilliant picnic food as it is equally great served hot or cold, but warm would always be my preference.

SERVES 8–10

✳

olive oil, for drizzling

12 large eggs

500g courgettes, grated, with excess moisture squeezed out

350g potatoes, parboiled, cooled and coarsely grated

1 bunch of spring onions, thinly sliced

1g (about a pinch) saffron threads, ground, then steeped in 2 tablespoons boiling water

2 tablespoons thick natural yogurt

2 tablespoons plain flour

2–3 teaspoons baking powder

2 heaped teaspoons sea salt flakes, crushed

freshly ground black pepper

Preheat the oven to 200°C, Gas Mark 6. Line a large rectangular or square ovenproof dish with baking paper, then drizzle a little olive oil on to the paper and rub it over the base. (Alternatively, use 2 smaller containers, or 16 muffin cases for individual kuku.)

Combine the eggs, courgettes, potatoes, spring onions, saffron, yogurt, flour, baking powder and salt in a large mixing bowl, season with black pepper and mix until evenly combined. Pour the mixture into the prepared ovenproof dish, ensuring the mixture is at least 2.5cm clear of the rim so it does not overflow during cooking. Bake for 35 minutes (or 25–28 minutes for smaller or individual kuku) or until the top of the kuku is golden and begins to brown. To check if it is cooked, insert a knife into the centre of the kuku – if it comes out clean of liquid (raw egg, in this case) but moist, the dish is done, if it looks wet and eggy then it will need a few more minutes.

Allow to cool slightly, then flip the baking dish upside-down and tip out the kuku on to a chopping board. Peel off the baking paper and cut the kuku into pieces to serve.

CHICKPEA & POTATO LATKES
with Mint & Chilli Salsa

I have always loved anything with grated potatoes – from my very first hash brown to the more continental rösti or a wonderfully crunchy potato latke. Here I have taken the basic method of a latke (combining grated potatoes with onions) and amped up the flavour with a little spice and the addition of spinach and chickpeas, which have a lovely crispy texture when fried. This is really great snack food, but equally good as part of a main meal, too.

MAKES 12–14
✳

300g potatoes
1 large onion, peeled
1 teaspoon coriander seeds
1 teaspoon cumin seeds
75g spinach leaves, very roughly chopped
400g can chickpeas, drained and chopped
2 garlic cloves, minced
finely grated zest of 1 lime
2 large eggs
1 heaped tablespoon plain flour
sea salt flakes and freshly ground
   black pepper
vegetable oil, for frying

For the mint & chilli salsa
½ red onion, very finely chopped
4 large, ripe tomatoes
1 small green chilli, very finely chopped
½ small packet (about 15g) of fresh
   coriander, leaves chopped
generous handful of mint leaves, chopped
1 tablespoon olive oil

Coarsely grate the potato and onion into a large mixing bowl. Add a generous pinch of salt and leave for 10 minutes until the salt draws out some of the liquids.

Meanwhile, lightly crush the coriander seeds and cumin seeds with a pestle in a mortar and set aside.

Place the potato and onion mixture in a sieve and squeeze to extract all the excess liquid until the mixture is very dry. Place the mixture back in the mixing bowl and add the ground seeds, spinach, chickpeas, garlic and lime zest and stir well.

Add the eggs, mix well, then add the flour, season with pepper and mix until everything is combined.

Heat some oil in a deep frying pan over a medium-high heat. Take handfuls of the mixture, squeeze out any excess liquid and flatten in your hands to make patties. Carefully drop these into the oil, 2 at a time, and shallow-fry for 1 minute on each side or until golden, crisp and cooked through. If the patties are browning too quickly, lower the temperature. Using a slotted spoon, remove the cooked patties from the oil and leave to drain on a plate lined with kitchen paper while you cook subsequent batches.

To make the salsa, put the onion in a mixing bowl and grate in the tomatoes, discarding the skins. Add the chilli and season with salt and pepper to taste. Add the chopped coriander, mint and the olive oil, then stir to mix well – the mixture will be quite loose. Serve with the latkes.

FETA BITES
with Preserved Lemon Jam

Call me biased but I love feta. I always say, 'Feta makes everything better' – I'm aware that rhyming doesn't help my cool factor, but feta is cheap, easy to find, incredibly versatile… need I say more? This recipe is fun and couldn't be simpler. The preserved lemon jam comes together in minutes and works incredibly well with the deep-fried salty feta. I kid you not – this delicious dish impresses everyone and is perfect for sharing.

MAKES 16

*

For the feta
vegetable oil, for frying
2 x 200g blocks of feta cheese, each cut into 8 cubes
150g self-raising flour, plus extra for dredging
1 egg
100ml ice-cold water

For the preserved lemon jam
6 preserved lemons (pick the largest ones in the jar), deseeded and finely chopped
6 tablespoons caster sugar

First, make the jam. Set a small saucepan over a medium heat. Put in the chopped preserved lemon and caster sugar, stir well and cook for 6–8 minutes until thickened. Take the pan off the heat and set aside.

Heat a saucepan over a medium-high heat and pour in the oil to a depth of 7cm.

Carefully dredge the cubes of feta in flour and dust off any excess flour.

In a measuring jug, whisk together the egg and the 100ml of cold water, then add the self-raising flour and mix very lightly. Avoid overmixing to whisk out lumps – it is the lumps that will keep the batter light.

I find it easier to batter the feta on the end of a skewer. Insert a skewer gently into the centre of each feta cube, dip the cube into the batter to coat it well, then slide the cube off the skewer into the hot oil and fry until the feta cube is golden brown on all sides. Immediately follow with as many other cubes as you can fit into the saucepan without overcrowding it. When cooked, drain on a plate lined with kitchen paper.

Spoon the preserved lemon jam into a suitable dish and serve alongside the feta, with a pile of cocktail sticks so that people can skewer and dunk the feta into the jam.

ZA'ATAR & GOATS' CHEESE PUFFS

This recipe is one of those great all-rounders – it's ideal as finger food, is wonderful for breakfast or brunch, and it makes a welcome change from a bread roll when served with soup or simply as a snack. However you serve it, expect a few to go missing once they come out of the oven because I find it hard to resist wolfing down a couple of piping hot ones as soon as they are cooked. These delicious cheese puffs can be reheated very easily – simply heat for 6 minutes in the oven at 180°C, Gas Mark 4 – or you can make up a batch and cook half straight away and refrigerate the rest to cook later.

MAKES 20

✳

1 x 320g ready-rolled puff pastry sheet (about 350 x 230mm)

olive oil, for brushing

2 heaped tablespoons za'atar

300g soft goats' cheese

sea salt flakes and freshly ground black pepper

Preheat the oven to 220°C, Gas Mark 7. Line a large baking tray with baking paper.

Lay the puff pastry sheet on a chopping board leaving its greaseproof liner underneath. Ensure the longer edges of the pastry rectangle are parallel with the edge of your work surface. Brush the pastry with just enough olive oil to lightly coat the sheet, then sprinkle 1 tablespoon of the za'atar evenly over the base.

Put the goats' cheese in a bowl and break it down using a fork. Distribute the cheese evenly over the pastry sheet, ensuring you leave a 2.5cm border at the longer edge of the pastry rectangle that is furthest from you. Season generously with salt and pepper, then sprinkle over the remaining za'atar.

Turn over the long edge of pastry that is closest to you and start to roll it up away from you – carefully roll up the pastry as tightly as possible without crushing it. Using a serrated knife, cut the roll in half and slice each half into 10 rounds. Pat each whirl flat to help them stay together during cooking, then place them on the prepared baking tray. Bake for 15 minutes or until golden brown. Serve immediately.

MUSHROOM, ARTICHOKE & FETA SWIRLS

This is a dish I first came up with to cater for a vegetarian who was attending one of my supper clubs. It was a simple, last-minute creation and, much to my surprise, turned out beautifully – so much so that, although I'm a meat-lover, I would be only too happy to have it as my main meal.

MAKES 6

✳

500g chestnut mushrooms, thinly sliced

500g artichoke hearts in oil

1 tablespoon thyme leaves, finely chopped

200g feta cheese

finely grated zest of 1 unwaxed lemon

6 sheets of filo pastry (each about 480 x 255mm)

beaten egg, to glaze

handful of sesame seeds

freshly ground black pepper

Preheat the oven to 220°C, Gas Mark 7. Line a large baking tray with baking paper.

To make the filling, heat a large saucepan over a high heat and add the mushrooms. Do not stir them for a couple of minutes, so that the intense heat of the pan dries out the moisture of the mushrooms first. Add 3–4 tablespoons of the artichoke preserving oil and stir the mushrooms quickly to prevent them from sticking, but once they have absorbed the oil, stop stirring and leave to fry for a few more minutes until cooked. Then stir the mushrooms again, add the chopped thyme, stir once more and transfer the mushrooms to a plate. Leave to cool slightly.

Drain the remaining oil from the artichoke hearts (keep it for making salad dressings) and roughly chop the artichoke hearts, ensuring the pieces are not too small, and place them in a mixing bowl. Crumble in the feta cheese, add the lemon zest and a generous seasoning of black pepper. Finally, add the cooled mushroom and thyme mixture and gently combine the ingredients using a fork (so as not to overly mash the mixture).

Lay a sheet of filo pastry on a clean work surface. Ensure the longer edges of the pastry are parallel with the edge of your work surface. Divide the filling mixture into 6 equal portions. Form 1 portion into a sausage shape along the long edge of the pastry sheet closest to you, leaving a 2.5cm border. Fold the corners of pastry closest to your body towards the centre, over the ends to secure the filling. Roll the long edge of pastry that is closest to you over the filling, then continue to roll up the pastry loosely, to encase the filling. Stop 5cm short of the end of the pastry sheet. Brush the end of the sheet with beaten egg, then continue to roll to the end of the pastry sheet.

Press the pastry together at either end of the roll to seal it. Now shape the tube into a tight coil, like a Moroccan m'hencha pastry. Place the coil on to the prepared baking tray and brush with beaten egg. Repeat with the remaining pastry sheets and filling. Sprinkle with some sesame seeds and bake for 25 minutes or until golden brown. Serve immediately.

VINE-BAKED FETA

Once you have tried quivering, molten feta with a delicious combination of flavourings, you might never go back to eating feta any other way. And you will also understand why I have stated that this recipe serves 2 when, technically, it could stretch to 4. If you really struggle to find vine leaves, don't worry – simply wrap up the cheese in some baking paper instead, much the way you would wrap a present. I like to serve these with flatbread.

SERVES 2

*

6–8 large vine leaves (vacuum packed or in brine)
200g block of feta cheese
1 unwaxed lemon
2 tablespoons garlic oil
1 teaspoon pul biber chilli flakes
leaves from 4 sprigs of fresh thyme or 1 teaspoon dried thyme

Preheat the oven to 220°C, Gas Mark 7. Line a baking tray with baking paper.

Lay out all but 1 of the vine leaves on a chopping board, ensuring they overlap one another slightly. Place the feta in the centre. Grate the lemon zest directly over the cheese, ensuring it falls evenly over the surface. Gently drizzle over the garlic oil, trying to keep it on the surface of the cheese, rather than allowing it to spill over the edges. Then sprinkle over the pul biber. Finally, sprinkle over the thyme leaves (or, alternatively, add whole sprigs, if you prefer).

Carefully wrap up the feta in the vine leaves to make a nice parcel and place the last remaining vine leaf on top to secure the parcel. Bake for 22–25 minutes. Serve the parcels whole and let your diners peel away the leaves at the table.

PAN-FRIED HALLOUMI

with Pomegranate Seeds, Pea Shoots & Pomegranate Molasses

Halloumi is an ingredient I always keep in my fridge. It has a long shelf life, stores easily and allows you to make a meal in minutes. This recipe is a great way in which to enjoy halloumi, with a few humble additions helping to give this wonderful cheese a real wow factor. Add some warm crusty bread to make a meal of it.

SERVES 2–4

✻

vegetable or light olive oil, for frying

500g halloumi cheese, cut into 1cm-thick slices

50g pea shoots

100g pomegranate seeds

4 tablespoons pomegranate molasses

1 teaspoon nigella seeds

olive oil, for drizzling

Heat a large frying pan over a medium-high heat. Once hot, drizzle in a little oil and fry the halloumi slices for approximately 1 minute on each side or until the slices have formed a deep golden brown crust.

Remove the halloumi from the pan and arrange on serving plates. Scatter over the pea shoots and pomegranate seeds, then drizzle over the pomegranate molasses. Finally, scatter over the nigella seeds, give the dish a scant drizzling of olive oil and serve.

PRESERVED LEMON & BAHARAT-MARINATED PORK LOIN KEBABS

Baharat is a Lebanese spice blend that can now (thankfully) be found in many supermarkets or online. The word *baharat* simply means 'spice', and the phrase is used in much the same way as *masala* is used in India and *adiveh* is used in Iran: to signify any type of spice blend. In many homes, there is a signature blend that is made in large batches for general use. You can, of course, make your own, but why do that when you can cheat and use baharat? Add that to a pork loin and you'll get a great flavour as it cooks in a smoking-hot griddle pan.

SERVES 4
*
400g pork fillet loin
vegetable oil, for drizzling

For the marinade
3 heaped tablespoons baharat spice blend
2 fat garlic cloves, peeled and crushed
3 tablespoons Greek yogurt
4 tablespoons olive oil
5 preserved lemons, deseeded and very finely chopped
sea salt flakes and freshly ground black pepper

Split the pork fillet lengthways and cut each half into cubes that measure roughly 3.5 x 3.5cm. Using a rolling pin, lightly beat each piece (2 hits, 1 on each side, will do the job) so that the proteins break down a little, then throw the meat into a mixing bowl. Add the baharat spice blend, garlic and yogurt and mix well with a spoon. Add the olive oil and a generous amount of salt and pepper, followed by the preserved lemons. Using your hands, really work the marinade into the pork for a few minutes. Once done, cover the bowl in clingfilm and refrigerate for a minimum of 1 hour or even overnight, if you like.

Bring the pork to room temperature. Heat a large griddle pan or heavy-based saucepan over a medium-high heat. Pierce about 3 or so pieces of the marinated pork on to a skewer and repeat until all the pieces of meat are skewered. Line up your skewers on a plate and drizzle with vegetable oil to prevent them sticking to the hot griddle pan. Place the skewered meat on to the griddle pan and grill for 2–3 minutes on each side or until all the kebabs are cooked through. (If you don't have skewers, grill the pieces of meat directly on the pan without moving them until they need to be turned.) Remove from the griddle pan, cover with kitchen foil and leave to rest for a few minutes, then serve.

MERGUEZ SAUSAGE ROLLS
with Almond, Pepper & Herb Paste

This is my take on the great British sausage roll. What's not to love about a sausage wrapped in flaky puff pastry? It makes perfect finger food. Merguez sausages are expertly spiced thin lamb sausages. They make a nice change from the ordinary and are great wrapped in pastry, too. As they are thinner and also leaner than pork sausages, I've spread a little paste inside the pastry to give additional flavour.

MAKES 18

*

100g almonds

2 tablespoons olive oil

750g–1kg thin lamb Merguez sausages

150g ready-roasted red peppers
    (from a jar), drained

1 tablespoon red wine vinegar

2 garlic cloves, crushed

handful of white bread (stale is ideal),
    soaked in 2 tablespoons milk until soft

½ small packet (about 15g) of flat leaf
    parsley, leaves finely chopped

1 x 320g ready-rolled puff pastry sheet
    (about 350 x 230mm)

beaten egg, to glaze

sea salt flakes and freshly ground
    black pepper

Preheat the oven to 180°C, Gas Mark 4. Line a large baking tray with baking paper.

Put the almonds in an oven tray and toast in the oven for 8–10 minutes until they take on a deep golden-brown colour, then set aside. Increase the oven temperature to 200°C, Gas Mark 6.

Heat a frying pan over a medium heat, drizzle in the oil and fry the Merguez sausages until just a little golden. Don't worry about cooking them all the way through as they will finish cooking in the oven later. Once done, lay them on some kitchen paper to absorb any excess grease. Trim and discard the ends of each sausage, then cut the sausages into 5cm lengths and leave to cool.

In a small food processor or using a hand-held blender, blitz the almonds, red peppers, vinegar, garlic and bread with a couple of good pinches of salt and a generous seasoning of pepper until the mixture forms into a paste. Transfer to a bowl and add the chopped parsley.

Lay your puff pastry sheet on a clean surface and use a rolling pin to gently roll it out as much as possible (without making it so thin that it tears). Cut the pastry into strips that are roughly 5cm wide and 7cm long (depending on the thickness of your Merguez – you want enough pastry to wrap around the Merguez halves, yet to leave the ends exposed). Spread just under 1 teaspoon of the paste on a pastry rectangle leaving a 1cm border, then place a Merguez half on the rectangle so that it is centred and the edges hang equally over the pastry edges. Wrap the pastry around the sausage, pinching the sides to seal, but leaving the ends of the tube open. Repeat until all the sausage halves and pastry have been used.

Place the rolls on to the prepared baking tray and brush with the beaten egg. Bake for 22–25 minutes or until the pastry has risen and the sausages are cooked through, then serve immediately.

LAMB LETTUCE WRAPS
with Peanut Sauce

Lettuce wraps are one of my all-time favourite things to eat. No matter what you fill them with, be it meat, poultry or vegetables, they hold both flavour and texture beautifully to give you the perfect mouthful. I especially love them as part of a meal with several other dishes, and because they are light you can afford to indulge without worrying about your waistline.

SERVES 4–6

✳

600g lean diced lamb leg
150ml dark soy sauce
6 tablespoons clear honey
4 teaspoons ground cinnamon
3 teaspoons ground cumin
2 fat garlic cloves, crushed
vegetable oil, for frying
leaves from 2 heads of round lettuce or 3 heads of gem lettuce

For the peanut sauce
400ml coconut milk
250g smooth peanut butter
2 tablespoons clear honey

To serve
unsalted peanuts, roughly chopped
4 spring onions, roughly chopped

Using a meat mallet or a rolling pin, flatten each piece of meat with a few hits. Place the meat in a mixing bowl. Add the soy sauce, honey, cinnamon, cumin and garlic and, using your hands, mix well so that the honey dissolves evenly into the mixture. Cover with clingfilm and leave in the refrigerator to marinate for 2 hours or overnight, if you wish.

To make the peanut sauce, heat a small saucepan over a medium-low heat. Pour in the coconut milk and add the peanut butter and honey. Bring to a gentle simmer, stirring constantly, until the peanut butter and honey dissolve into the coconut milk.

Heat a large frying pan over a medium-high heat to cook the meat. Drizzle in a little vegetable oil and, shaking off any excess marinade, fry the lamb slivers in the pan, ensuring you don't overcrowd the pan.

Meanwhile, gently reheat the peanut sauce until warm.

Serve the meat on a platter with the lettuce leaves, peanuts and spring onions and the peanut sauce in a bowl. To assemble a wrap, take a lettuce leaf, place some lamb on top, drizzle with peanut sauce and top with nuts and spring onions. Roll up and enjoy.

LOQMEH (MOUTHFUL) SPICED LAMB KEBABS

Who doesn't love a kebab? These are really easy to make and can be served as a starter, finger food or as a main meal. To assemble the kebabs, the meat and accompaniments are rolled up in tortilla quarters – either serve them assembled ready-to-eat or, as this is a great meal to share with friends, lay out the various elements of the dish and let your guests help themselves.

SERVES 4

✳

vegetable oil, for frying

1 large onion, finely chopped

500g minced lamb

2 teaspoons turmeric

2 teaspoons ground cumin

2 teaspoons ground cinnamon

For the yogurt sauce

200g Greek-style yogurt

2 tablespoons ground coriander

squeeze of lemon juice

4 tablespoons olive oil

sea salt flakes and freshly ground
   black pepper

For the harissa oil

1 teaspoon rose harissa

1 tablespoon olive oil

To serve

4 tortilla wraps (or more, if desired),
   each cut into quarters

½ small packet (about 15g) of fresh
   coriander, roughly chopped

4 spring onions, thinly sliced

Combine all the ingredients for the yogurt sauce in a small bowl, seasoning to your liking, and mix well.

In a very small bowl, dilute the harissa in the olive oil to make the harissa oil. Set aside.

To cook the lamb mince, heat a large frying pan over a high heat and drizzle in enough vegetable oil to coat the base of the pan. Fry the onion until golden brown, then add the minced lamb and mix well to break down the meat and combine it with the onion. Add the turmeric, cumin and cinnamon and mix well until the spices evenly coat the meat. Cook for 8–10 minutes until the meat is brown and cooked through, then take the mixture off the heat and set aside.

To assemble the kebabs, spoon 1–2 tablespoons of the lamb on to each quarter of tortilla, add a dollop of yogurt, a little drizzle of harissa oil, sprinkle over some fresh coriander and spring onion and serve.

LAMB, APRICOT & FENNEL SEED LOLLIPOPS

Call these lollipops, kofta or meatballs (which is, technically, what they are), they make quite a statement when served. In all fairness, you can ditch the wooden skewers and serve them as they come, but putting them on sticks adds to the fun. The 'lollipops' are great as party food or as part of a big meal, and I've found that they are enjoyed by kids and adults alike. I mean, who doesn't like a meatball? Seriously.

MAKES 18–20

500g minced lamb

150g ready-to-eat dried apricots, finely chopped

50g fennel seeds, toasted and finely ground

2 large eggs

1 onion, minced in a food processor or very finely chopped

2 heaped teaspoons turmeric

½ small packet (about 15g) of dill, finely chopped, plus extra to garnish

2 heaped teaspoons sea salt flakes, crushed

freshly ground black pepper

vegetable oil

To serve

150g Greek yogurt

olive oil or lemon juice (optional)

sweet tamarind sauce

small handful of nigella seeds

Heat a large frying pan over a medium heat (or a high heat, if using an electric cooker). If your frying pan isn't large enough to cook 18–20 kofta at once without overcrowding the pan, preheat the oven to 160°C, Gas Mark 3 for keeping cooked batches warm.

Put all the kofta ingredients, except the oil, into a large mixing bowl and work the mixture thoroughly using your hands. Really pummel the meat mixture and ensure the ingredients are evenly combined.

Drizzle into the hot frying pan just enough oil to coat the base and allow it to heat up. Meanwhile, begin rolling your kofta – take a small amount of the meat mixture (about the size of a ping pong ball) and roll it into a smooth ball, then place it in the frying pan and fry for about 5–6 minutes on each side or until nicely browned and cooked through. Keep adding more and more balls as you make them, cooking in batches if necessary. Keep the cooked kofta warm in the oven on a baking tray while you fry subsequent batches.

Season the yogurt with salt and pepper. If the yogurt is too thick for drizzling, thin it down using a little olive oil and 1 tablespoon water or lemon juice.

Arrange the kofta on a large platter and pour over a generous drizzle of the seasoned yogurt, followed by a drizzle of sweet tamarind sauce and a sprinkling of nigella seeds. Insert a wooden skewer into each meatball and serve.

STICKY LAMB BUNS
with Pickled Cucumber Relish

Ever wondered what to do with leftover roasted meat? This is the quick and easy answer you were looking for. I first came up with this recipe when stuck with a lamb shoulder all to myself due to a friend cancelling on lunch at the last minute. What to do? As hungry as I usually am, not even I can eat 2.5kg lamb shoulder in one sitting and, once it got cold, it needed a little magic to bring it back to life again and make it finger-licking good. If you don't have bread rolls, make open sandwiches or tortilla wraps. The recipe works well with leftover pork or chicken, too.

SERVES 4

✳

600g picked roast lamb shoulder, shredded

2 teaspoons rose harissa

6 tablespoons clear honey

1 heaped teaspoon ground cumin

2 heaped teaspoons ground cinnamon

4 bread rolls, toasted (if desired) just prior to serving

sea salt flakes

For the pickled cucumber relish

½ large cucumber

½ red onion, finely diced

2 tablespoons rice vinegar

2 heaped teaspoons caster sugar

1 teaspoon sesame oil

1 teaspoon nigella seeds

handful of dill, fronds finely chopped

100g pomegranate seeds

To make the relish, quarter the cucumber lengthways into 4, then thinly slice and place in a bowl along with the diced onion. Season with a few generous pinches of salt. Mix well and allow to rest for 15 minutes. Now stir again and leave to sit for another 15 minutes. After the resting time, drain off any excess moisture from the mixture and wrap it in a clean tea towel or a few sheets of kitchen paper until nice and dry.

Place the cucumber and onion mixture in a bowl, add the vinegar, sugar and sesame oil and mix well until the sugar has dissolved and the marinade coats the cucumber and onion. Then add the nigella seeds, dill and pomegranate seeds and set aside.

Put the shredded meat into a saucepan set over a medium heat, add the harissa, honey, cumin and cinnamon and coat the meat in the mixture. (You can slacken the mixture with a little oil, water or even apple juice, 1 tablespoon at a time, to soften the texture.) Season with salt to taste and, once the consistency has reached a moist and juicy meat mixture, remove from the heat. Serve inside the bread rolls with a generous amount of relish.

QUINCE-GLAZED CHICKEN FILLET SKEWERS

Membrillo, or Spanish quince paste, is a wonderful product to keep in the cupboard. Traditionally served with cheese, I can easily think of dozens of other ways to use it, from making marinades to Martinis – it really is versatile. This quick and very delicious glaze for chicken is, well, just a bit different. Skewered, served with salad or stuffed into bread, the chicken is great however you serve it.

SERVES 2 AS A MAIN MEAL OR 4 AS PART OF A FEAST

✳

125g Membrillo

100ml good-quality apple juice (preferably cloudy)

2 tablespoons olive oil, plus extra for frying

½ teaspoon ground cinnamon

1 teaspoon ground ginger

400g mini chicken fillets or chicken breast, cut into 2.5cm-thick strips

sea salt flakes and freshly ground black pepper

To make the glaze mixture, put the Membrillo, apple juice, olive oil and spices into a medium-sized bowl, season generously with salt and pepper and mix well until the Membrillo is broken down and the mixture is smooth. Mix in the chicken strips, then cover with clingfilm and allow to marinate in the refrigerator for at least 1 hour (although you can fry the strips immediately if you don't have time to marinate).

Heat a large frying pan over a medium heat, drizzle in enough oil to coat the base of the pan then, using tongs, place the marinated chicken strips into the pan (not too close together) and fry them for a few minutes on each side until nicely browned all over and cooked through. As the glaze contains sugar, the chicken may blacken as the sugar caramelizes, but that is OK.

Once cooked, pierce with skewers and serve.

ORANGE, THYME & SPICE CHICKEN WINGS

I could eat chicken wings all day long until I keel over. Spicy ones, sticky ones, zingy ones, herby ones, grilled, fried or roasted, I don't discriminate – I love them all. They are cheap, delicious and great for sharing. I really like this fruity marinade, which has a little spice and thyme to help round off the flavour. The longer you marinate the chicken wings in it, the better they will taste. If you are anything like me, you will double the batch and continue eating them the next day.

SERVES 4

✳

1kg chicken wings (or use drumlets)

For the marinade
200ml fresh orange juice
6 tablespoons marmalade
4 heaped teaspoons dried thyme
2 heaped teaspoons ground cinnamon
1 heaped teaspoon turmeric
1 teaspoon cayenne pepper
2 fat garlic cloves, minced or crushed
3 tablespoons olive oil
sea salt flakes and freshly ground black pepper

Put the chicken wings in a large bowl.

Combine the marinade ingredients in a small bowl, seasoning very generously with salt and pepper, then pour the mixture over the chicken wings. Using your hands, massage the marinade into the chicken wings, then cover the bowl with clingfilm and refrigerate for at least 3 hours or, even better, overnight.

When you are ready to cook, bring the chicken wings to room temperature. Preheat the oven to 200°C, Gas Mark 6. Line a large baking tray with baking paper.

Place the chicken wings on the prepared baking tray (reserve the excess marinade) and roast on the top shelf of the oven for 25 minutes. Turn over the chicken wings and, using a teaspoon, drizzle over some of the reserved marinade. Continue to roast for another 25 minutes or until the chicken wings are deeply browned and cooked through (keep in mind that the sweet marinade will make them blacken a little around the edges, which is perfectly OK).

Set a small saucepan over a high heat, pour in the leftover marinade and bring to the boil. Cook for a few minutes until reduced to a sauce-like consistency – if it becomes too thick, let it down with a tablespoon of water – then serve on the side.

SPICY TURKEY LETTUCE WRAPS

Lettuce wraps are a great way to enjoy leftovers and pack lots of flavour into fun morsels. You can use any kind of meat for these wraps, but I do love turkey mince as it's incredibly lean and a great vehicle for wonderful flavours. My nephews Cyrus, Darius, Kasra and Dastan literally wolf these down and create their own flavour combinations using different toppings and sauces. This recipe is a winner for kids and adults alike and all you need to do is fry the mince, which takes minutes! Perfect for a quick midweek supper or weekend feast.

SERVES 2–4

✳

vegetable oil, for frying

2 heaped teaspoons coriander seeds

4 garlic cloves, crushed

2 generous thumbs of fresh root ginger, peeled and finely chopped

2 long red chillies, deseeded if preferred, and finely chopped

finely grated zest of 2 limes

500g minced turkey

½ small packet (about 15g) of mint, leaves rolled up tightly and thinly sliced into ribbons

sea salt flakes and freshly ground black pepper

To serve

½ small packet (about 15g) of fresh coriander, leaves and stems finely chopped

100g peanuts (or your favourite nut), roughly chopped

10 radishes, sliced into 2.5mm slices, then sliced into matchsticks

1 bunch of spring onions, thinly sliced

1 large head of iceberg lettuce, halved, leaves carefully separated to use for wraps

2 limes (use the ones you zested earlier), cut into wedges

150ml your favourite chilli sauce or sweet chilli sauce

Set a large frying pan over a medium heat, then drizzle in a little vegetable oil and add the coriander seeds. Stir for 1 minute or so until the seeds begin to pop, then add the garlic, ginger and chillies and stir-fry until the ginger softens. Increase the heat a little, add the lime zest and turkey mince and fry the mince until cooked through. Season well with salt and pepper to taste, remove from the heat and stir in the fresh mint.

Serve the mixture alongside the fresh coriander, peanuts, radishes, spring onions, lime wedges and chilli sauce, and use the lettuce leaves as wraps.

MARINATED SCALLOPS

with Lime, Chilli & Shallot Dressing

Scallops are one of my favourite things to cook when I want to create a special menu for friends and family. If you buy really fresh scallops, there is no need to cook them as their delicate, sweet flesh will be delicious and, with a simple dressing, they can carry some pretty explosive flavours. And the best thing of all? No pans to wash. And I can promise you there won't be any leftovers, either.

SERVES 2

✳

8 very fresh large raw scallops, corals/roe removed

For the dressing
1 teaspoon sumac
finely grated zest and juice of 1 lime
3 tablespoons olive oil
2 sprigs of dill, fronds and stems finely chopped
2 round shallots, very finely diced
1 long red chilli, deseeded and finely diced
1 teaspoon caster sugar

Using a sharp knife, cut each scallop thinly into 3 slices and place them in a bowl.

To make the dressing, mix the sumac with the lime zest and juice and the oil in a small bowl. Add the dill, shallots, chilli and sugar and stir vigorously until the sugar dissolves.

Pour the dressing over the scallops, coating each slice well. Arrange on a platter, pour over any remaining dressing and serve.

EASTERN-STYLE SALMON TARTARE

I first fell in love with salmon tartare when I was served it, in a mini cone, at a Thomas Keller restaurant. Keller's dish was minced and refined, unlike the chunkier versions I had eaten previously and had not much love for, so I developed my own version. This was the first course of the first supper club I hosted so it has special memories for me. What I like about this dish is that you can really pack a lot of flavour into it and, better still, it doesn't require any cooking. I tend to keep salted tortilla chips in my cupboard on standby, which, when served with this dish, make it great for sharing... but you might find you're not in a sharing mood once you've tasted it.

SERVES 6

✳

400g best-quality salmon loin (use a trusted fishmonger)

finely grated zest of 2 limes and juice of ½

4 tablespoons extra virgin olive oil

2 heaped teaspoons sumac

1 heaped teaspoon nigella seeds

1 small red onion, very finely diced

½ small packet (about 15g) of dill, finely chopped

½ small packet (about 15g) of fresh coriander, finely chopped

sea salt flakes and freshly ground black pepper

Using a sharp knife, cut the salmon into thin strips and dice them up. Then finely mince the salmon with the knife until very fine.

Put the minced salmon in a bowl. Add the lime zest, olive oil, sumac, nigella seeds, red onion and herbs and mix thoroughly. Season generously with salt and pepper. Lastly, add the lime juice, mix thoroughly again and adjust the seasoning if necessary. This dish is great served with lettuce leaves used as wraps, tortilla chips or simply on its own with a wedge of lime.

TAMARIND HONEY PRAWNS

Iranians love all things sour: lemons, limes, pomegranate molasses, young plums and tamarind. I especially love tamarind because you can use it so well in savoury cooking and balance it with sweetness to create something really delicious. In this recipe, I simply mix tamarind paste with honey to make a marinade that has lots of flavour without much effort. These prawns are also great to skewer and are easy to cook on the barbecue.

SERVES 4–6

✳

800g raw tiger prawns (the biggest you can find), ideally peeled but with tails left on
vegetable oil, for frying
2 heaped teaspoons toasted sesame seeds
10g fresh coriander, leaves roughly chopped
3 spring onions, thinly sliced from root to tip

For the marinade
100g tamarind paste
75g clear honey
2 garlic cloves, peeled and crushed
2 tablespoons light brown sugar
3–4 tablespoons chilli oil (or olive oil, if preferred)
sea salt flakes

To prepare the marinade, thoroughly blend the ingredients in a mixing bowl until the sugar dissolves. Add the prawns and work the marinade into them using your hands. Cover the bowl with clingfilm and allow to marinate at room temperature for 30 minutes.

Heat a large frying pan over a medium-high heat and drizzle in a little vegetable oil. Drain any excess marinade from the prawns, then fry them quickly on both sides until they are cooked through and slightly charred. Cooking times will vary depending on the size of the prawns – if using standard supermarket prawns, you won't need to cook them for more than 1 minute or so each side. But if you are using larger, meatier prawns, you may need to reduce the heat slightly and allow them to cook for a little longer. The marinade is sticky and sweet, which means it will blacken in the pan slightly, so don't panic if the prawns look charred – they will still taste delicious. Serve sprinkled with toasted sesame seeds, coriander and chopped spring onions.

*

spectacular salads & sides

MARINATED KALE
SALAD *page 136*

CANTALOUPE, FETA, GREEK BASIL
& PUMPKIN SEED SALAD *page 112*

STIR-FRIED GREEN
BEANS *page 158*

EASTERN SLAW *page 134*

QUINCE-GLAZED CHICKEN
FILLET SKEWERS *page 94*

APPLE, SUMAC, RED ONION & POMEGRANATE SALAD

Apples can be such a refreshing addition to salads, but in this instance they are the main attraction. Their sweet yet sharply acidic flavour makes them incredibly versatile and a great accompaniment to spices, herbs and bold, savoury flavours. There are many different varieties of apple to choose from, but time and again I turn to Braeburns, as their texture, flavour and balanced sweetness suits my preferences perfectly. But, of course, you can go rogue and select your favourite variety.

SERVES 6

✳

4 Braeburn apples
olive oil, for drizzling
juice of 1 large lemon
3 teaspoons coarse sumac (finely ground, powdery sumac will dye your salad pink)
1 small red onion, halved and thinly sliced into half moons
200g pomegranate seeds
20g mint, leaves roughly chopped
sea salt flakes and freshly ground black pepper

Leaving the skin on, roughly dice the apples into 1cm cubes as best you can, discarding the cores and seeds. Place the apple cubes in a mixing bowl. Drizzle with some olive oil and pour over the lemon juice, which will prevent the apple from oxidizing and turning brown.

Add the sumac and red onion slices and mix well. Season with just a little salt and some pepper, add the pomegranate seeds (but not the juices) and the chopped mint and mix well. Serve immediately.

CANTALOUPE, FETA, GREEK BASIL & PUMPKIN SEED SALAD

For me, melon and watermelon are the taste of summer. Watermelon and feta are a long-embraced combination, and this is my version using honey-sweet orange-fleshed cantaloupe melon and a little kick of chilli, with tiny yet pungent Greek basil leaves. It is well worth waiting for the melons to come into season to enjoy this dish – and enjoy it several times while they are available.

SERVES 2–4

✳

1 large cantaloupe melon or other orange-fleshed melon

150g feta cheese

extra virgin olive oil, for drizzling

1 teaspoon pul biber chilli flakes

75g pumpkin seeds

generous handful of Greek basil leaves

Using a sharp knife, cut the melon into quarters, then cut each quarter in half (this will make removing the skin much easier). Slide the base of a sharp knife under the melon's flesh, against the skin, to cut the flesh away from the skin. Slice each wedge into 2 thinner slices. Arrange the melon slices on a platter.

Crumble the feta cheese over the melon slices, then drizzle with a little olive oil. Sprinkle the pul biber and pumpkin seeds over the feta, scatter the Greek basil leaves liberally over the melon and serve.

DATE, ORANGE, ALMOND & WATERCRESS SALAD

Dates have a jammy, intense sweetness that really do need a kick of acid to complement them. This salad is packed full of flavours that work well with the dates, from the refreshing sweet flavour of the orange to the crunch of the almonds. But what really makes this dish for me is the salad dressing: a cinnamon vinaigrette. It doesn't sound like it should work, but it really brings it all together brilliantly.

SERVES 4

✳

3 oranges

100g watercress

150g Medjool dates, pitted, each sliced into 4 pieces

50g toasted almonds

For the dressing

2 tablespoons clear honey

2 tablespoons red wine vinegar

4 tablespoons olive oil

scant ½ teaspoon ground cinnamon

sea salt flakes and freshly ground black pepper

You'll need a sharp knife to peel the oranges. Cut a round disc of peel off the top and base of the orange. Then, working from the top of the fruit downwards, cut away the remaining peel and pith in strips until the entire orange is peeled. Cut the oranges in half across the middle and cut them into slices that are just less than 1cm thick – you'll get roughly 5 slices per orange half.

Arrange the watercress, orange slices and dates on a plate and sprinkle over the toasted almonds. Combine the dressing ingredients in a jug, drizzle over the salad and serve immediately.

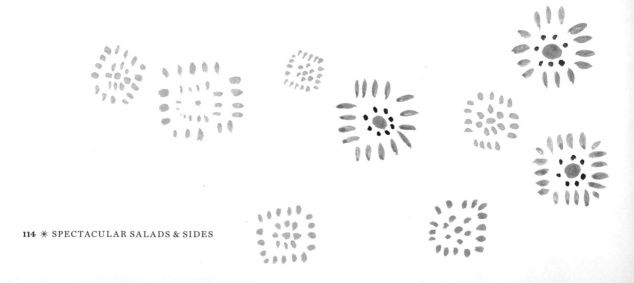

GRILLED PEACH & GEM LETTUCE SALAD

with Honey Lime Dressing

This salad is simple enough, but the charred peaches really give it an added dimension. It is thought that kebabs originated in ancient Persia when Persian soldiers would set up camp and use their swords to roast or grill meat. The word 'kebab' (or kabaab, as it is pronounced in Persian) refers to anything roasted or grilled. In the Middle East, we seem to roast many a pepper, aubergine and tomato, but I really love roasting fruits and more unusual vegetables. This dish is great served with grilled halloumi, fish or chicken.

SERVES 4

✳

2 large peaches, halved, stoned and cut into 6 wedges

4 heads of baby gem lettuce, halved

olive oil, for brushing

½ red onion, thinly sliced into half moons

75g flaked almonds

20g chervil, roughly chopped

1 teaspoon sumac

sea salt flakes and freshly ground black pepper

For the honey lime dressing

2 heaped tablespoons clear honey

juice of 1 lime

2 tablespoons extra virgin olive oil

1 tablespoon cold water

Preheat a griddle pan over a high heat.

Combine the dressing ingredients in a bowl or jug and mix well until evenly combined. Set aside.

Brush the peach wedges and the cut sides of the gem lettuces generously with olive oil. Place the gem lettuce halves on the hot griddle pan, cut-sides down, and grill for 2 minutes, then set aside. Now grill the peach wedges for 2 minutes on each side (or more, if needed) until char marks appear, then remove from the heat.

Arrange the gem lettuce halves, grilled peach wedges and red onion slivers on serving plates or one large platter. Scatter over the flaked almonds, chervil and sumac and season well with salt and pepper. Pour the dressing over the salad and serve.

FIG, FRESH PECORINO & WALNUT SALAD
with Mixed Leaves & Balsamic Vinegar

When I make salads, I often want them to be more of a meal than just a few leaves and this dish is one such example. I'm mad about figs and think they work really well in salads, especially when salty cheese and aged, syrupy balsamic vinegar are both present. A young, fresh pecorino that is semi-soft with a creamy texture (usually found in delis) is worth the trouble taken to find.

SERVES 4

✳

4 figs

100g mixed baby salad leaves or Continental/herb leaves

300g young, fresh pecorino cheese (or use feta cheese)

75g walnuts, broken into pieces

extra virgin olive oil, for drizzling

4 tablespoons thick, aged balsamic vinegar

good handful of mint leaves, roughly torn

freshly ground black pepper

Remove the stalks from the figs and quarter them.

Arrange the salad leaves and fig quarters in a large shallow bowl or on a platter. Crumble the cheese over the leaves and scatter over the walnut pieces.

Pour a good drizzle of olive oil over the salad, followed by the balsamic vinegar. Season with a good grinding of black pepper, scatter over the torn mint leaves and serve.

RADISH, DRIED FIG & APPLE SALAD

I love combining the intense, concentrated sweetness of dried fruit with a sharp burst of fresh fruit. Such a marriage works very well in this refreshing salad, which has lots of texture and crunch. It goes especially well with red meats, cutting through richness with its acidity. It looks incredibly beautiful, too, which isn't a bad thing either.

SERVES 6–8

*

250g dried figs, stalks removed, quartered

2 Braeburn apples, quartered, cored and thinly sliced

150g radishes, thinly sliced

200g pomegranate seeds

2 tablespoons olive oil

4 tablespoons pomegranate molasses

100g mixed leaves

Combine the fig, apple and radish slices and the pomegranate seeds in a large mixing bowl. Dress them with the olive oil and pomegranate molasses and toss to coat everything in the dressing. Add the leaves to the dressed ingredients and mix again – there should be sufficient dressing to coat the leaves without making the salad too mushy. Serve piled high on a flat platter.

MAFTOUL SALAD

Maftoul (Palestinian couscous) is still relatively unknown in the West and I am determined to share my love of it with you. The word *maftoul* means hand-rolled or twisted, referring to the method in which these irregularly shaped wholegrain pearls are made. I love using maftoul in salads and stuffings. This particular recipe is now a firm favourite of mine and I play with the ingredients quite a lot, but here is the original (and best) version of the recipe.

SERVES 6
✳

250g maftoul
olive oil, for drizzling
finely grated zest and juice of 1 orange
finely grated zest and juice of 1 lemon
400g can chickpeas, drained
200g ready-to-eat dried apricots, thinly sliced
100g dried sour cherries, roughly chopped
1 bunch of spring onions, thinly sliced
1 black garlic bulb, cloves peeled and thinly sliced
50g flat leaf parsley, leaves finely chopped
2 heaped teaspoons ground cinnamon
sea salt flakes and freshly ground black pepper

Boil the maftoul in plenty of boiling water according to the packet instructions. Drain, rinse with cold water and leave to stand until all the excess water has drained.

Put the maftoul into a large mixing bowl and drizzle generously with olive oil. Add the orange and lemon zest and juices with a generous amount of salt and pepper and mix well. Add the remaining ingredients and gently fold them into the maftoul. Cover the bowl with clingfilm and leave to rest for 1 hour (ideally in the refrigerator) to allow the flavours to infuse. Remove it from the refrigerator and leave to stand at room temperature for 30 minutes before serving.

FREEKEH SALAD

Freekeh is one of my favourite things ever. I only discovered it a few years ago and have fallen for it big time. It's a smoked green wheat that, because it is picked when the wheat is young (and green), has a completely different nutritional profile to traditional wheat – and the smoking gives it an incredible, delicious flavour. This particular recipe is my party trick. It's the salad I make when I am asked to bring along a dish as it looks beautiful and tastes wonderful. Thankfully, supermarkets are now beginning to stock freekeh, which hopefully means that it will soon be a kitchen staple for us all.

SERVES 6–8

✳

500g freekeh

1 small red onion, very finely diced

250g dried cranberries

200g blanched almonds

20g dill, fronds and stems finely chopped

50g fresh coriander, leaves and stems finely chopped

400g pomegranate seeds

150ml pomegranate molasses

generous glug of olive oil

Bring a large saucepan filled with hot water from a kettle to a boil and cook the freekeh according to the packet instructions. Drain the freekeh, rinse thoroughly until cold and place it in a large mixing bowl.

Add the remaining ingredients to the bowl with the freekeh and give everything a thoroughly good mix. Cover with clingfilm and allow to rest for 1 hour before serving.

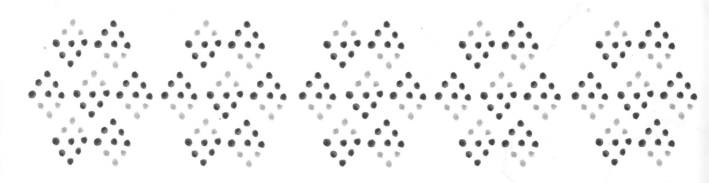

WARM SALAD OF SPICED KALE, BULGAR WHEAT & PUY LENTILS

I like to add serious amounts of spice to robust green leaves such as kale, because they can stand up to bold additions – much in the way that meat can. Not only is this salad full of flavour, it is also very healthy. You don't need to add anything to it, but some grilled chicken or fish would really make a meal of it.

SERVES 2 AS A STARTER OR 4 AS A MAIN MEAL

*

100g dried Puy lentils

100g bulgar wheat

olive oil, for frying

1 heaped teaspoon cumin seeds

6 fat garlic cloves, bashed and
    thinly sliced

2 long red chillies, thinly sliced

400g kale, stalks removed,
    leaves roughly torn up

2 teaspoons ground turmeric

2 teaspoons ground cumin

1 teaspoon ground cinnamon

finely grated zest of 2 unwaxed lemons
    and juice of 1

2–3 generous handfuls of pumpkin seeds

100g feta cheese, crumbled

sea salt flakes and freshly ground
    black pepper

lemon wedges, to serve

Boil the Puy lentils and bulgar wheat separately according to the packet instructions, then rinse immediately under cold water until cold. Drain well, then combine them in a large mixing bowl.

Set a large saucepan over a medium-high heat, drizzle in a little olive oil, then add the cumin seeds. Once the seeds begin to sizzle and pop, add the garlic and the chilli slices and stir well, ensuring the garlic doesn't burn.

Meanwhile, wash the kale leaves and drain, without shaking off excess water (which will add moisture during the cooking process). Set aside.

When the garlic has sweated and is translucent, add the dry spices and lemon zest and stir well. Add a little more oil if the spices dry up too much. Add the slightly wet kale to the pan (it should sizzle) and stir for 1 minute to ensure the garlic and spice mixture coats the leaves well. Cover the saucepan with a lid and allow the contents to steam for 2 minutes. Stir well again and take the pan off the heat. Replace the lid for another couple of minutes.

Lift off the saucepan lid and transfer the contents of the pan to the bowl containing the Puy lentil and bulgar wheat. Give the ingredients a good mix, pour in the lemon juice, season generously with salt and pepper and add a little extra drizzle of olive oil, if desired. Check the seasoning and adjust if necessary, then stir in the pumpkin seeds. Transfer to a large serving platter. Crumble the feta cheese over the top and serve with lemon wedges.

CHICKPEA, RED ONION & PARSLEY LEAF SALAD

Herbs are used as a garnish in so many dishes, but the milder leaves, such as parsley, also make wonderful bases for salads. I love parsley salads and make many different varieties. This one is nice and simple and makes a great accompaniment to any meal.

SERVES 4

*

100g flat leaf parsley, large stems thinly sliced

1 small red onion, halved and thinly sliced into half moons

400g can chickpeas, drained and rinsed

6 preserved lemons, deseeded and roughly chopped

6 pickled red chillies

extra virgin olive oil, for drizzling

juice of ½ lemon

freshly ground black pepper

Choose a nice wide platter and scatter over the parsley sprigs and chopped stems to cover as much of the platter as possible. Scatter the red onion on top, followed by the chickpeas, preserved lemons and the pickled chillies. Drizzle generously with some olive oil (you won't need any salt as the preserved lemons will season everything beautifully for you), squeeze over the lemon juice and season with a little freshly ground black pepper to finish. Serve immediately.

PUY LENTIL, CAPER & RED ONION SALAD

Pulses are a big deal in my household so I always have six or seven varieties in my cupboard, at any time. Puy lentils are one of my favourite. Small but mighty, they have a wonderful texture and flavour and hold their shape beautifully, making them perfect for salads.

SERVES 6

✳

250g Puy lentils

3 tablespoons red wine vinegar

4 tablespoons olive oil

3 tablespoons sumac

3 teaspoons sea salt flakes

1 large red onion, finely diced

140g drained capers

50g flat leaf parsley, leaves and stems finely chopped

freshly ground black pepper

Cook the lentils according to the packet instructions, then drain and rinse under cold water.

Put the lentils in a large bowl and add the vinegar, olive oil, sumac and salt. Season generously with black pepper. Mix together, allowing the lentils to absorb the dressing. Add the red onion, capers and parsley and give everything a good mix.

Cover the bowl with clingfilm and leave to rest in the refrigerator for 1 hour before serving. The salad is best enjoyed at room temperature.

WHOLEGRAIN BASMATI RICE GREEK-STYLE SALAD

Greek salad is the salad that makes the most regular appearance in my home. I always have feta in my fridge, so pulling it together is very easily done and provides the perfect pairing with any meat or fish. Although Greeks only use vinegar when making this salad, I like to use lemon juice more than anything else. But what further deviates from the authentic *horiatiki* is my addition of brown rice, which happened by accident one day when I didn't want to make a separate rice dish to accompany the salad, so I made a more substantial meal of it by adding wholegrain basmati rice – then wondered why I hadn't done so sooner.

SERVES 8–10

✳

300g wholegrain basmati or brown rice

400g feta cheese, cut into small cubes or broken into small chunks

1 large red onion, finely diced

1 cucumber, cut into 1cm cubes

600g baby plum/cherry tomatoes, halved

150g Kalamata olives, pitted

20g dill, leaves and stems finely chopped

20g mint, leaves finely chopped

4 tablespoons dried oregano

finely grated zest and juice of 2 lemons

olive oil, for drizzling

sea salt flakes and freshly ground black pepper

Boil the rice in plenty of boiling water according to the packet instructions. Drain the rice and rinse it under cold water, then drain it again and place it in a large mixing bowl.

Add the remaining salad ingredients to the mixing bowl and drizzle with a generous amount of olive oil, season with salt and pepper and mix well again. Check the seasoning and serve immediately. I find that this salad is best eaten immediately but, of course, it will also be fine the next day – just a tad more watery. To remedy this, discard any excess liquid and drizzle over a little more olive oil to give the leftovers a new lease of life.

BLACK & WHITE RICE SALAD

with Chicken & Mango

I literally can't think of a single type of rice that I don't like. From basmati to bomba, I enjoy every single grain, variety and colour of the stuff – hot, cold, sweet or savoury. Rice salads have a special place in my heart because there is always leftover rice in my house and, when it doesn't get 'egg-fried', it gets turned into a salad with any nuts, seeds, dried fruit or herbs that are knocking about. They are perfect for a colourful feast or just something different in your lunch box. This one is as delicious as it is striking.

SERVES 6–8

✳

500g basmati and wild rice (usually available uncooked and ready-mixed in a packet)

1 small cooked chicken or 4 cooked chicken breasts, flesh picked and shredded

2 large ripe mangoes, diced roughly into 1cm chunks

1 large red onion, sliced into wafer-thin half moons

2 long red chillies, deseeded and finely chopped

50g fresh coriander, leaves and stems finely chopped

20g mint, leaves finely chopped

½ red cabbage, halved, cored, outer leaves removed, halved again and thinly sliced

2 yellow peppers, cored, deseeded and cut into thin strips

couple of handfuls of golden raisins (optional)

olive oil, for drizzling

finely grated zest and juice of 2 limes

4 tablespoons clear honey

sea salt flakes and freshly ground black pepper

Boil the rice in plenty of boiling water according to the packet instructions. Drain the rice and rinse it under cold water, then drain it again and place it in a large mixing bowl.

Add the chicken and the remaining ingredients to the mixing bowl with a generous drizzle of olive oil, salt and pepper, then mix well before serving.

EASTERN SLAW

I love coleslaw... yes, even that bizarre version served up as part of school dinners in the Eighties – I always ate it all up. It was creamy, exotic and totally different to anything I had experienced in my single-digit years. But oh – how coleslaw has come along over the years! The 'cole' part of the word seems to have been ditched entirely in favour of the more trendy 'slaw'. And so many versions have now joined the mainstream, from crunchy Asian slaw with soy sauce and sesame oil to healthier versions that omit mayonnaise entirely. Well, flavour rather than health is the focus of my recipes, and this one is most definitely delicious. Try splitting open a baguette and piling in some chicken or turkey slices with a generous amount of slaw to make a great, crunchy sandwich.

SERVES 4–6

✳

4 tablespoons Greek yogurt

2 tablespoons mayonnaise

1 heaped tablespoon cream of horseradish

2 teaspoons ground coriander

1 teaspoon ground cinnamon

1 heaped teaspoon nigella seeds

generous handful of golden raisins

½ white cabbage, thinly shredded

¼ cauliflower, stalk removed, florets thinly sliced

1 large fennel bulb, quartered and thinly sliced, fronds chopped

1 red onion, very thinly sliced into half moons

2 apples (of your choice), quartered, cored and thinly sliced

20g mint, leaves roughly chopped

20g dill, fronds and stems roughly chopped

sea salt flakes and freshly ground black pepper

Put the yogurt, mayonnaise, horseradish, coriander, cinnamon and nigella seeds into a small bowl and stir well. Add the golden raisins, season generously with salt and pepper and mix well.

Put the vegetables and apples into a large bowl and pour over the sauce. Use your hands to ensure everything is well coated and evenly mixed. Add the fresh herbs, mix well again until the ingredients are evenly combined and serve.

MARINATED KALE SALAD

Because kale is rather good for you, it seems to be taking over the world lately – but I have been eating it for years as its robust leaves make a great alternative to cabbage in a roast dinner. Admittedly, how I eat kale has changed – everything from kale stir-fries to kale chips is now on the menu, and I am always coming up with new and interesting ways to enjoy it. This dish has to be one of my favourite uses for kale. Why? Well, there's no cooking involved, it's quick, easy and inexpensive to make, and it is delicious.

SERVES 4–6

＊

200g kale, stalks removed

2 teaspoons ground cinnamon

2 tablespoons sumac

50g flaked almonds

50g sunflower seeds

sea salt flakes and freshly ground black pepper

For the dressing

1 Braeburn apple, cored and cut into rough dice

10cm piece of fresh root ginger, peeled and roughly chopped

1 tablespoon clear honey

1 tablespoon chilli sauce

3 tablespoons light soy sauce

1 tablespoon olive oil

1 tablespoon sesame oil

juice of ½ lime

Using a hand-held blender or a mini food processor, blitz the dressing ingredients until the mixture is smooth and evenly combined.

Put the kale into a large mixing bowl and pour over the dressing along with the cinnamon, sumac and a good seasoning of salt and pepper. Use your hands to work the dressing into the kale thoroughly, which will wilt the leaves a little. Once wilted, add the flaked almonds and sunflower seeds and combine well. Cover the bowl with clingfilm and refrigerate for 1 hour before serving.

CARROT, TAHINI & TOASTED HAZELNUT SALAD
with Mint

I love salads with ample crunch, texture and dimension, and this delicious dish hits all these notes. It's a great year-round salad, but also works really well as a slaw, of sorts, jammed into a sandwich with any type of leftover meat. The final touch of mint gives the dish the perfect hint of freshness to offset the rich nutty tahini and sweet crunch of carrots.

SERVES 4

✳

500g carrots, peeled and thinly sliced diagonally

1 large red onion, halved and thinly sliced into half moons

100g toasted hazelnuts, roughly halved or chopped

40g mint, leaves finely chopped

For the dressing

2 tablespoons tahini

4 tablespoons olive oil

finely grated zest and juice of 1 lemon

2 tablespoons cold water

sea salt flakes and freshly ground black pepper

Put the carrots, red onion, hazelnuts and mint in a bowl and mix well.

To make the dressing, put the tahini, olive oil, lemon zest and juice and the 2 tablespoons of water (which is added to slacken the mixture) in a small bowl and stir well. Season generously with salt and pepper. Pour over the salad, tossing it through to coat the vegetables well. Serve immediately.

PRAWN, TENDERSTEM BROCCOLI, FETA & ALMOND SALAD

I absolutely love broccoli and wouldn't usually think to pair it with seafood, but the combination works well. There is so much flavour and texture in this salad that it is terribly moreish. This dish works well as a starter, for lunch or as part of a main meal. I can happily eat half of it in one sitting, then save the other half to eat on the following day. It's a great salad for picnics, too, because even when chilled, it is really quite satisfying.

SERVES 4–6

✳

100g blanched almonds

400g Tenderstem broccoli

400g raw, large Madagascar prawns,
    peeled but with tails left on

finely grated zest of 2 unwaxed lemons

1 heaped teaspoon rose harissa

4 tablespoons olive oil

200g block of feta cheese

20g dill, fronds and stems finely chopped

For the dressing

4 heaped tablespoons clear honey

juice of 1½ lemons

2 tablespoons olive oil

sea salt flakes and freshly ground
    black pepper

Preheat the oven to 190°C, Gas Mark 5. Line a baking tray with baking paper.

Place the almonds on the prepared baking tray and toast them in the oven for 10 minutes, then remove and set aside.

Bring a large saucepan of water to the boil and blanch the broccoli for 5 minutes. Drain and plunge the broccoli stems into cold (but not iced) water to arrest cooking. Drain and set aside.

Combine the dressing ingredients in a bowl, seasoning well with salt and pepper, and set aside.

Heat a griddle pan over a high heat. Place the prawns in a large bowl, add the lemon zest, rose harissa and olive oil, season well with salt and work the mixture into the prawns. Leave the prawns to marinate for a few minutes, then lay them on the hot griddle pan and cook for 2 minutes on each side or until they turn pink and are cooked through. Remove the prawns from the heat.

Choose a nice large platter and arrange the broccoli and prawns on it. Crumble over the feta cheese and scatter the almonds on top. Give the dressing a final stir and drizzle it over the salad. Scatter over the chopped dill and serve.

SWEET POTATOES
with Baked Feta

Sweet potatoes are one of my favourite root vegetables. Mashed, steamed, fried or baked, that killer sweet flavour is right up my street. The addition of feta reminds me of Greece and makes a fabulous condiment for the sweet potatoes. It's such a good combination that you'll find yourself eating double the amount you bargained for. You have been warned!

SERVES 4–6

✳

1.5kg orange-fleshed sweet potatoes, peeled and cut into thick wedges

4–5 tablespoons garlic oil

200g block of feta cheese

3 teaspoons dried oregano

2 tablespoons Greek yogurt

sea salt flakes and freshly ground black pepper

Preheat the oven to 220°C, Gas Mark 7. Line both a large and small baking tray with baking paper. Fold a double layer of kitchen foil into a rectangle and place this in the small tray – this will serve as a base on which your block of feta will sit.

Place the sweet potato wedges on to the prepared large tray. Pour over the garlic oil and season generously with salt and pepper. Using your hands, toss the sweet potato wedges in the oil to ensure each piece is coated.

Roast the sweet potatoes for 20 minutes. Place the block of feta on the foil base on the small baking tray and pop this into the oven to bake alongside the sweet potatoes but, before closing the oven door, turn the sweet potatoes over. Cook for a further 10–12 minutes or until tender and the edges of the sweet potatoes are burnished and nicely browned. Set aside the sweet potatoes.

Place the softened baked feta in a small heatproof bowl, add 2 teaspoons of the oregano and the Greek yogurt and mix well. Arrange the wedges on a platter then, using a teaspoon, dollop the feta here and there over the sweet potatoes. Sprinkle over the remaining oregano and serve.

CUMIN-ROASTED AUBERGINE WEDGES

with Pumpkin Seeds, Pine Nuts, Pomegranate & Yogurt Dressing

For Middle Eastern people, the aubergine is a diet staple. While we don't really embrace it as a salad item in the West, I think it makes a wonderful salad ingredient, whether it is grilled, fried, preserved or – in this case – roasted. Roasting aubergines in the oven is a healthier way of cooking as it uses less oil than frying and allows you to celebrate the flavour in a concentrated form. I can happily eat this dish on its own, on my own, but it's a great one for sharing as it's a real crowd-pleaser.

SERVES 6–8

✳

3–4 large aubergines, cut into wedges (ensure the skin sides are 5cm wide)

100–150ml olive oil

5 teaspoons cumin seeds

6 tablespoons Greek-style yogurt

4–5 tablespoons pomegranate molasses

75g toasted pine nuts

50g pumpkin seeds

½ small packet (about 15g) of fresh coriander, leaves and stems finely chopped

100g pomegranate seeds

sea salt flakes and freshly ground black pepper

Preheat the oven to 220°C, Gas Mark 7. Line a large baking tray with baking paper.

Using a pastry brush, brush the exposed flesh sides of each aubergine wedge with a good amount of olive oil. Arrange the wedges, skin-sides down, on the prepared baking tray, then sprinkle liberally with the cumin seeds, ensuring some seeds land on the exposed flesh of the wedges. Roast for 45–60 minutes or until the aubergine wedges are golden brown, with dark, burnished edges. Arrange the wedges on a large, flat platter and season well with salt and pepper.

Give the yogurt a good seasoning of salt and pepper and dilute it with a little water if it is too thick to drizzle. Drizzle the yogurt over the aubergines, followed by the pomegranate molasses. Sprinkle liberally with the toasted pine nuts and pumpkin seeds, followed by the chopped coriander. Lastly, sprinkle over the pomegranate seeds and serve immediately. If you have leftovers, they are great eaten the next day, served at room temperature.

TURMERIC & SPICE-MARINATED CAULIFLOWER

with a Rich Tomato Sauce

Cauliflower is so versatile. It's crunchy and almost a little spicy when raw, yet comforting and mild when cooked. It's a great carrier of flavour and can hold its own against bold spicing, as it does in this deliciously rich tomato sauce. Marinating it is a wonderful way to impart deep flavour to the florets and frying it retains its texture, but adds a nice crunchy element, too.

SERVES 6

✳

6 tablespoons olive oil

2 garlic cloves, finely chopped

400g can chopped tomatoes

1 heaped teaspoon sugar

1kg cauliflower or 850g prepared
   cauliflower florets

1 teaspoon turmeric

1 teaspoon ground cumin

1 teaspoon ground coriander

1 teaspoon ground ginger

½ teaspoon smoked paprika (pimentón)

finely grated zest and juice of 1 lemon

vegetable oil (approximately 750ml),
   for frying

150g Greek yogurt

½ small packet (about 15g) of fresh
   coriander, leaves finely chopped

1 teaspoon nigella seeds

sea salt flakes and freshly ground
   black pepper

Heat a saucepan over a medium heat, add 2 tablespoons of the olive oil and sauté the garlic until it browns. Mix in the chopped tomatoes, add the sugar and a generous amount of salt and pepper, reduce the heat to low and cook gently for about 30 minutes or until the sauce is thick and concentrated. Turn off the heat.

If using a whole cauliflower, peel away the leaves and trim off any excess stalk, then cut the head into small florets without discarding the stalks. Combine the spices with the lemon zest and juice and the remaining olive oil in a large bowl, then add the cauliflower and rub the paste all over the florets. Leave to marinate for 20 minutes.

Pour the vegetable oil into a large wok, frying pan or saucepan and heat over a medium-high heat ready for frying. Meanwhile, line a large tray or plate with kitchen paper. Cooking in batches, carefully lower the cauliflower florets into the hot oil using a metal slotted spoon and fry them for approximately 6 minutes or until they are deep golden brown all over (remember that the colour of the spices will make them look a lot darker than they actually are). Remove from the oil with a slotted spoon, allowing the oil to drain off the cooked florets, then transfer to the paper-lined tray or plate to allow excess oil to be absorbed by the kitchen paper.

Reheat the tomato sauce. Spoon the cauliflower on to serving plates and drizzle the tomato sauce all over the florets, followed by generous dollops of Greek yogurt. Scatter over the chopped coriander, then the nigella seeds, and serve.

CRUSHED NEW POTATOES

with Garlic, Dill, Chargrilled Spring Onions & Peas

We don't really use potatoes very often in Iran, but having grown up in England, I have a lot of loyalty to the humble spud. It is cheap, versatile and can be a meal in itself (think jacket potatoes) or make a great side dish. I am not entirely sure how to classify this dish, to be perfectly honest with you, but for me, it is the taste of spring. While technically a side dish, I have eaten it happily as my main meal without any accompaniments. Although, thinking about it, crispy bacon on top would be devilishly good…

SERVES 6

✳

2 bunches of spring onions

olive oil, for drizzling

750g new potatoes

75g salted butter, cubed

20g dill, fronds and stems finely chopped

2 large garlic cloves, crushed

150g fresh peas

sea salt flakes and freshly ground black pepper

Preheat a griddle pan or frying pan over a high heat. Preheat the oven to 220°C, Gas Mark 7. Line a baking tray with baking paper.

Bring a saucepan of water to the boil over a medium-high heat and blanch the spring onions in the water for 2 minutes, then drain and place them on kitchen paper to drain off any excess moisture. Drizzle the spring onions with a little of the oil and place them on the hot griddle pan. Sear them for a couple of minutes on each side until they are charred. Remove from heat and set aside.

Put the whole potatoes on to the prepared baking tray, drizzle generously with olive oil and season with salt and pepper. Using your hands, toss the potatoes to coat them in the oil and seasoning. Roast for 30–40 minutes (depending on the size of the potatoes) or until they are cooked through.

Place the potatoes in a mixing bowl with the butter. Using a fork, roughly break up the potatoes to a coarse 'crush' without mashing them to a purée. Add the dill, crushed garlic and raw fresh peas and gently fold them in. Add a little more salt and pepper according to preference and a drizzle of olive oil.

Cut each of the spring onions in half and fold them into the crushed potatoes. Serve immediately.

SOUK-SPICED ROOTS

I absolutely love root vegetables. They can really hold a great deal of spice and are comforting at any time of year. The truth is, when I cook, I like to go big. So if you want to cater for a smaller number, simply halve this recipe. If, like me, you like leftovers, they can be blitzed with some vegetable stock to make a lovely soup. Alternatively, mash them a little and turn them into root vegetable cakes, then fry until crisp. This dish is great with red or white meats and fish alike, and is fabulous with a little crumbled feta.

SERVES 6-8

✳

2 teaspoons cumin seeds

2 teaspoons ground coriander

1 teaspoon ground cumin

1 teaspoon turmeric

1 teaspoon ground cinnamon

1 teaspoon cayenne pepper

1 teaspoon garlic granules

1 head of celeriac

750g large parsnips

1kg carrots (I like to use a mix of orange and purple carrots, when in season)

olive oil, for drizzling

sea salt flakes and freshly ground black pepper

Preheat the oven to 220°C, Gas Mark 7. Line 2 large baking trays with baking paper.

Combine all the spices and the garlic granules in a small bowl and set aside.

Peel the root vegetables, then cut them into similar-sized shapes. I find that starting with the celeriac and cutting it into generous 5cm pieces helps me to gauge how to cut the rest of the vegetables. But don't stress too much about the way in which you cut them – roughly the same size and shape is fine, so they will cook at the same rate. In the worst-case scenario, you can always cook one variety longer than another, if needed.

Lay the roots on the prepared baking trays and drizzle generously with olive oil. Season with a generous amount of salt (I'd recommend using several teaspoons of sea salt flakes, as roots are sweet and need to be seasoned properly) and ground black pepper, too. Sprinkle the spice mixture liberally over the oil-drizzled roots and, using your hands, toss the roots well in the oil and spices, ensuring each piece is evenly coated. Roast for approximately 50 minutes; after 20 minutes of this cooking time has elapsed, allow steam to escape from the oven by opening the door and then closing it again. The vegetables are ready when they are tender and nice and brown around the edges.

CARAMELIZED FENNEL

with Coriander Seeds, Orange & Saffron Butter

During my career, I have converted many a fennel-hater with recipes that show that the flavour of fennel is much milder and more complex than you might expect. The flavours of coriander and saffron in this dish complement the aniseed character of fennel beautifully, and this simple recipe makes the perfect accompaniment to fish or white meat. Having said that, it is also great as a starter by itself.

SERVES 4

✳

3 large fennel bulbs, quartered, stalks trimmed

2 tablespoons icing sugar

olive oil, for frying

For the sauce

1 heaped teaspoon toasted coriander seeds, lightly crushed using a pestle and mortar

50g salted butter

good pinch of saffron threads

finely grated zest and juice of 1 unwaxed orange

sea salt flakes and freshly ground black pepper

Heat a large frying pan over a medium heat.

Dip the cut sides of the fennel quarters in the icing sugar to give them a good coating. Dust off any excess sugar.

Drizzle a little olive oil into the warm pan and gently cook the coated sides of the fennel quarters for a few minutes until caramelized. Then turn the pieces to expose the curved sides to the heat and cook for 1 minute. Remove from pan and arrange on a platter.

To make the sauce, put the coriander seeds into the same pan and increase the heat to medium-high. Add the butter and saffron and mix well. Once the butter melts and begins to bubble, add the orange zest and juice, season generously with salt and pepper and continue to cook, stirring. Once the saffron bleeds and colours the sauce deeply, take the pan off the heat and, using a teaspoon, drizzle the sauce over the caramelized fennel. Serve immediately.

ASPARAGUS
with Preserved Lemon & Pickled Chilli

I love asparagus in every which way it is prepared – grilled, steamed, boiled, roasted... it's all good to me. You don't even need to turn on the hob to prepare this super-simple dish, yet it packs in so much flavour. Any tasty meal that can be pulled together this quickly using just a few store cupboard ingredients has got to be a good thing.

SERVES 4

✳

300g asparagus tips, trimmed

4 large preserved lemons, deseeded and finely chopped

6 pickled chillies, thinly sliced

½ small packet (about 15g) of mint, leaves picked, rolled up and sliced into ribbons

freshly ground black pepper

olive oil, for drizzling

Put the asparagus into a shallow bowl and pour over enough to boiling water from a kettle to cover them. Leave to sit for 5 minutes. Drain the hot water and place the bowl under running cold water to cool the asparagus. Once cooled, dry the excess moisture from the spears using kitchen paper.

Halve the asparagus spears lengthways and place them in a bowl. Add the preserved lemons, pickled chillies, fresh mint and a generous amount of black pepper, then drizzle with some olive oil. Mix well and serve.

SLOW-ROASTED CHERRY TOMATOES

with Goats' Curd, Pine Nuts & Grape Molasses

Iranians love roasting whole tomatoes. They are skewered and placed straight on to a grill, then blistered until blackened, which adds so much flavour. They are traditionally served with kebabs, but goats' cheese and roasted tomatoes has to be one of my all-time favourite pairings. As goats' cheese can sometimes be strong in flavour, I'm using the far milder and more delicate goats' curd here, which doesn't detract from the wonderful taste of the tomatoes, then topping them with crunchy toasted pine nuts and grape molasses (which is a bit like pomegranate molasses but far less acidic). Here's a tip: if you like roasted tomatoes, double up on the volume, then refrigerate half the quantity of cooked tomatoes covered in a little oil in an airtight container for another day.

SERVES 4–6

✳

600g cherry tomatoes, halved

2 teaspoons dried oregano

extra virgin olive oil, for drizzling

300g goats' curd

50g toasted pine nuts

3 tablespoons grape molasses or pomegranate molasses

sea salt flakes and freshly ground black pepper

Preheat the oven to 140°C, Gas Mark 1. Line a large baking tray with baking paper.

Place the cherry tomatoes, cut-side up, on to the tray and sprinkle with the oregano. Roast for 2 hours without oil. I find that dressing them with oil once cooked allows you to get away with using a lot less oil and gives the tomatoes a nice, chewy texture, too.

Once cooked, plate up the tomatoes and season well with salt and pepper to taste. Drizzle generously with olive oil and, using a teaspoon, dollop the curd over the tomatoes. Scatter the pine nuts on top, then drizzle the grape molasses over to finish.

STIR-FRIED GREEN BEANS

I've never been one to turn my nose up at a healthy side of greens at any meal – in Iran we have the rice dish called *lubya polow,* in which green beans are the star of the show, as well as green bean *khoresh* (stew). But I also love green beans in salads, tarts and stews and find they can really stand up to spice in a way you wouldn't expect. This is a recipe for a pickle of sorts, made into a paste that works brilliantly with the beans. Serve this dish with meat, fish or poultry or just by itself.

SERVES 4–6

✳

4 garlic cloves, thinly sliced

6–8 pickled red chillies, sliced

4 preserved lemons, deseeded and finely chopped

20g fresh coriander, leaves roughly chopped

2 heaped teaspoons sugar

1 tablespoon red wine vinegar

2 heaped teaspoons turmeric

400g fine green beans, trimmed

olive oil, for frying

1 teaspoon mustard seeds

sea salt flakes and freshly ground black pepper

Using a pestle and mortar, make a paste with the garlic, pickled chillies, preserved lemons, coriander and sugar. Grind down the mixture as best you can without being overly pedantic. Then add the vinegar and turmeric and stir well. Set aside.

Heat a large saucepan over a high heat. Wash the trimmed beans and drain, without shaking off too much of the excess water. Drizzle enough olive oil into the hot pan to coat the base and add the mustard seeds (which will start popping wildly), then immediately add the beans, giving them a quick stir as they sizzle. Cover the pan with a lid and cook for 1 minute, then give the pan a shake to keep the beans moving. Lift off the lid, add the paste with a good seasoning of salt and pepper to taste and stir-fry the beans with the paste for 1 minute, stirring well to coat them evenly in the mixture. Replace the lid and allow to steam-fry for 2 minutes, giving the pan a shake a couple of times during this time. Remove the lid, stir the beans well and try one to ensure it is cooked, then serve immediately.

mouthwatering
main dishes

LAMB LETTUCE WRAPS
page 86

SPICE-ROASTED DUCK
page 178

BUTTER BEAN & ZA'ATAR DIP
page 52

CRUSHED NEW POTATOES
page 148

CHICKPEA, BUTTERNUT SQUASH, PRESERVED LEMON & HARISSA TAGINE

There are not many vegetarian dishes that leave me feeling truly satisfied but, time and again, this tagine has won me over, as well as even the most carnivorous of my friends, family and clients. It's a flavour-packed, one-pot-wonder that you can serve with rice, couscous or bread. Salt, heat, sour and sweet...what's not to love?

SERVES 4–6

✳

olive oil, for frying
2 onions, diced
4 garlic cloves, peeled and thinly sliced
2 heaped teaspoons ground cumin
1 heaped teaspoon ground cinnamon
1 heaped teaspoon ground turmeric
1 butternut squash, peeled and diced into 3.5cm cubes
2 heaped tablespoons harissa
3 tablespoons clear honey
2 x 400g cans chopped tomatoes
600g can chickpeas
250g ready-to-eat dried apricots
8 preserved lemons, some halved, some sliced widthways, or a squeeze of lemon (optional)
sea salt flakes and freshly ground black pepper
handful of chopped flat leaf parsley, to garnish

Set a very large saucepan over a medium heat, add a good amount of olive oil (enough to liberally coat the base) and sauté the onion and garlic until they are translucent and just begin to colour. Add the cumin, cinnamon and turmeric and stir well, incorporating the spices into the onion. Cook out the spices for a few minutes. Next, add the diced butternut squash and coat evenly with the spiced onion mixture. Cook for a few minutes, stirring well to stop the squash sticking to the pan.

Next, add the harissa and honey and, again, stir well to ensure they are evenly incorporated. Add the chopped tomatoes and, if desired, refill one of the tomato cans with water and add to slacken the mixture. Season with a generous amount of salt and some pepper. Add the chickpeas along with their canning water, stir well, then cook for 30 minutes, stirring occasionally.

Once the cooking time has elapsed, stir the contents of the pan, checking to see if the butternut squash is cooked through. Taste the tagine and adjust the seasoning, if desired, then add the apricots and preserved lemons or lemon juice and cook for a further 15–20 minutes. Stir, then garnish with chopped parsley and serve. Absolutely delicious.

AUBERGINE, PEPPER & TOMATO STEW

Another great stew to make in advance because it tastes even better with time. This one is perfect for vegetarians, but flavourful enough to satisfy meat-lovers too. The flavours are familiar and simple, but the gentle addition of spices and fresh herbs really gives it an edge.

SERVES 6–8

✳

olive oil, for frying

4 large or 6 small aubergines, peeled and cut into 2.5cm cubes

2 large red peppers, deseeded and cut into 1cm-thick strips

2 large green peppers, deseeded and cut into 1cm-thick strips

2 large onions, chopped into 1cm dice

5 fat garlic cloves, thinly sliced

2 teaspoons ground coriander

2 teaspoons ground cumin

2 tablespoons tomato purée

400g large ripe tomatoes, halved and roughly diced

400g can chopped tomatoes

1 heaped teaspoon caster sugar

sea salt flakes and freshly ground black pepper

small packet (about 30g) of flat leaf parsley, roughly chopped (optional)

small packet (about 30g) of fresh coriander, roughly chopped (optional)

Heat a large saucepan over a medium-high heat and pour in enough olive oil to generously coat the base of the pan. Start by frying your diced aubergines until the pieces begin to brown but not burn, adding a little more oil if needed. Once done, top up the pan with a little more oil, add the peppers and onions and fry until they soften.

Add the garlic slices and mix well. Now add the ground coriander and cumin and the tomato purée, stir well and cook out the flavours a little. Pour in the chopped fresh and canned tomatoes and another generous slug of olive oil. Mix everything together, season generously with salt and pepper and add the sugar, which balances the acidity of the tomatoes. Stir again, cover the pan with a lid, reduce the heat to the lowest possible setting and allow to slow-cook for about 1 hour or until the aubergine is soft. Stir through the chopped herbs if using, then serve immediately.

PERSIAN 'ADASSI' LENTIL STEW

This is a hearty dish that we Iranians enjoy in the cold and snowy winters of Iran, although I first ate it in Switzerland when my Aunty Nini cooked it for me. Her version, which I have been cooking for more than 20 years, is another great one-pot dish. The amount of flavour, considering how few ingredients are involved, always surprises me. It gets better and better the longer you keep it, as the flavours intensify. You can eat it as a soup, or make it thicker for a stew. Serve with crusty bread and enjoy.

SERVES 4

*

3 tablespoons vegetable oil

1 large onion, finely diced

300g green lentils

4 tablespoons tomato purée

2 heaped tablespoons medium curry powder

sea salt flakes

1.5 litres (or so) hot water from a kettle

Heat a saucepan over a medium-low heat (or a medium heat, if you are cooking on an electric hob). Add the oil and fry the onion until translucent. Add the green lentils and stir for 1 minute, then stir in the tomato purée, curry powder, season with salt, and add a couple of tablespoons of water to hydrate the mixture a little (spices absorb moisture quickly). Stir well for about a minute until the ingredients are evenly mixed in.

Then, in stages, stir in a few ladlefuls of hot water at a time, stirring well and allowing each ladleful of water to be thoroughly absorbed by the lentils before adding the next. Once all the water has been absorbed, taste the lentils to check you are happy with the texture and that they are cooked thoroughly. If not, add another 1–2 ladlefuls of water until you are satisfied.

GEORGIAN CHICKEN STEW

The flavour of this dish is unique, with a subtle hint of spice and lots of fresh herbs, making it the kind of thing I can wolf down in large quantities. Georgian food is simple, delicate in flavour and totally moreish and delicious. I eat this comforting stew with rice, bread or potatoes – it is a household staple now, especially when I'm feeling under the weather. This dish is great with rice or bread.

SERVES 4
*

olive oil, for frying
8 large chicken thighs, skin removed
2 large white onions, cut into 5mm half moons
4 bay leaves
4 garlic cloves, finely chopped
2 heaped teaspoons paprika (not smoked)
6 large ripe tomatoes, roughly chopped
3 tablespoons white wine vinegar
2 long red chillies
small packet (about 30g) of fresh coriander, leaves finely chopped
small packet (about 30g) of flat leaf parsley, leaves finely chopped
small packet (about 30g) of tarragon, leaves finely chopped
sea salt flakes and freshly ground black pepper

Heat a large pan over a medium heat, then drizzle in enough olive oil to coat the base of the pan well. Add the chicken thighs and fry until golden brown. Add the onions, bay leaves, garlic, paprika, tomatoes and vinegar and mix well. Season generously with salt and pepper. Split the chillies lengthways, keeping the stalks intact, and add them to the pan. Using boiling water from a kettle, top up the pan with just enough hot water to cover the chicken, then reduce the heat and simmer for 2 hours (uncovered), stirring occasionally. Top up with more water if necessary during cooking.

Check and adjust the seasoning as necessary, then add the chopped fresh herbs, stir well and serve.

CHICKENBERRY RICE

The Persian Empire influenced much of the cuisine of India's Mughal Empire. The Indian emperor Shah Jahan employed cooks from Persia who used huge volumes of saffron, dried nuts and dried fruits, as well as their signature steam-method that Persians still use to cook rice today. No dish of that era could be more famous than biryani, which is served all over India, Pakistan and the West. This version uses chicken breast, which because it is off the bone, cooks in half the time of a traditional biryani, so makes a great midweek supper.

SERVES 6

vegetable oil, for frying

2 large onions, halved and thinly sliced
   into half moons

8 green cardamom pods

1 teaspoon cumin seeds

small pinch (about 0.5g) of Iranian
   saffron threads

5 chicken breasts, cut into 5cm chunks

2 tablespoons Greek yogurt

500g basmati rice

generous handful of barberries

100g dried blueberries

100g dried cranberries

100g toasted almonds

75g pistachio slivers

sea salt flakes and freshly ground
   black pepper

Heat a saucepan over a high heat, then pour in enough vegetable oil to generously coat the base of the pan. Fry the onions until golden brown and crispy. Reduce the heat to medium, add the cardamom, cumin and saffron and stir well, then add the chicken breast chunks. Quickly seal the pieces of chicken breast (cook the outsides, leaving the insides raw), then stir in the yogurt. Season generously with salt, then take the pan off the heat.

Heat a large saucepan over a high heat, fill it with boiling water from a kettle and salt the water generously with a handful of sea salt flakes. Add the unwashed rice (you will wash it later) and parboil for 6 minutes. Have a large colander ready in the sink. Empty the parboiled rice into the colander and wash it thoroughly with cold water, using your hands to ensure every grain is thoroughly rinsed of starch. Drain the rice really well, shaking off excess moisture and leave it to stand for about 10 minutes.

Rinse the pan you used for the rice and dry it. Take a large square of baking paper and scrunch it into a ball, then carefully open it out and use it to line the base and sides of your pan to prevent the rice from sticking. Drizzle in enough vegetable oil to generously coat the base of the pan and sprinkle the base evenly with a little salt. Now begin layering – scatter a 1cm-thick layer of rice into the lined saucepan. Divide the chicken mixture into 3 equal portions and add 1 portion in an even layer over the rice. Follow this with generous amounts of the berries and nuts. Continue to layer the rice, chicken mixture and berries (reserving a little rice for the top) until they are used up. Scatter the reserved rice on top.

Using the handle of the wooden spoon, stab a series of holes into the layers, piercing right the way down to the base of the pan (this allows the steam to circulate), then wrap the pan lid in a tea towel (to lock in the steam and make a tight seal), cover the pan and cook the rice over the lowest temperature

possible if using gas, or a medium-low heat if using electric, for 45–60 minutes. A direct gas flame may burn the base of the rice dish – to avoid this, I would recommend you use a diffuser between the flame and the pan if you have one, in which case, double the cooking time. If you are lucky, you will get a nice crunchy crust.

My Persian roots dictate that I must always lift off the saucepan lid, lay a large platter over it and carefully flip the rice on to the platter to see how the crunchy base (*tahdig*) has turned out. Of course, you can simply spoon out the rice and pile it high on to a platter or shallow bowl and sneak most of the crunchy base as the chef's perk – I won't tell.

CHICKEN & APRICOT STEW
with Preserved Lemon, Harissa & Eggs

I love boiled eggs on pretty much anything, especially in curries and wet dishes in which there is a sauce to eat with them. This wonderful dish has layers of flavour and texture that all contribute to making it a new favourite for me. Whether it's summer or winter, this is definitely weekend comfort food to share with friends. And you won't need to make a ton of side dishes as it really has so much going for it already. My favourite accompaniment is basmati rice, flatbread, couscous or potatoes.

SERVES 4

✳

vegetable oil, for frying

2 onions, sliced into 5mm half moons

8 large bone-in chicken thighs, skin removed

2 teaspoons ground turmeric

2 teaspoons ground ginger

1 teaspoon ground cinnamon

2 teaspoons harissa

3 tablespoons clear honey

3 heaped teaspoons sea salt flakes, crushed

4 large eggs

50g breadcrumbs

8 preserved lemons, some halved, some sliced

16 ready-to-eat dried apricots

100g toasted chopped hazelnuts

20g flat leaf parsley, leaves finely chopped

freshly ground black pepper

Heat a large saucepan over a medium heat, drizzle in enough oil to coat the base of the pan and fry the onions for a few minutes until beginning to soften. Add the chicken thighs and combine with the onions, then add the dry spices, harissa and honey, stirring well. Season with the salt and some pepper, then add just enough boiling water from a kettle to barely cover the chicken thighs. Give everything a good stir, then cover the pan with a lid and cook for 1½ hours.

Toast the breadcrumbs, either in a preheated oven, 180°C, Gas Mark 4, for 8 minutes, or in a hot frying pan until they are golden brown. Set aside.

After the cooking time has elapsed, add the preserved lemons and apricots to the stew, stir well and cook with the lid off for a further 30 minutes. Turn off the heat, cover the pan with a lid and allow the stew to rest for 10 minutes before serving.

Meanwhile, heat a saucepan over a medium heat, then pour in hot water from a kettle. When the water is boiling gently, carefully add the eggs and boil for 6 minutes. Drain and immediately plunge the eggs into iced water to cool them enough to allow you to shell the eggs.

Halve the eggs and lay them gently on top of the stew. Combine the toasted hazelnuts with the breadcrumbs and chopped parsley, sprinkle the mixture on top and serve.

CITRUS & ZA'ATAR CHICKEN

Roast chicken is the ultimate comfort food, and I have been known to conjure up many different versions over the years. While I love a classic salt-and-pepper seasoned bird, I'm pretty adventurous and unafraid of throwing the contents of my spice racks and store cupboards at a chicken to liven it up when the mood suits. Za'atar is a staple spice blend in my house – it's so versatile, it goes with everything, and the fragrance of citrus zest really lifts this flavoursome dish. Try it: it's a winner. And don't waste the leftover fruits – juice them and add water and sugar to sweeten for a refreshing drink.

SERVES 3–4

✳

1 free-range chicken, about 1.5–1.75kg

3–4 tablespoons olive oil

2 heaped tablespoons za'atar

finely grated zest of 2 unwaxed lemons

finely grated zest of 2 unwaxed oranges

1 teaspoon turmeric

1 teaspoon ground coriander

1 teaspoon sea salt flakes, crushed

freshly ground black pepper

Preheat the oven to 220°C, Gas Mark 7. Line a roasting tin with baking paper. Place the trussed bird into the prepared roasting tin.

Put the olive oil in a small bowl, add the za'atar, citrus zests, turmeric, coriander, salt and a generous seasoning of black pepper and mix to make an evenly combined paste. Work the paste on to the chicken, rubbing it in all over it and between the breast and leg joints. Roast the chicken for 1½ hours or until the juices run clear when the thickest part of the thigh is pierced with a skewer. Leave to rest for 10 minutes, then serve.

SPICE-ROASTED DUCK

What the Chinese don't know about duck simply isn't worth knowing. I have loved crispy duck and pancakes since I was a child and I enjoy the way it is served, with lots of little accompaniments alongside the pancakes. As long as the duck is crispy and the fat has rendered, no matter what you serve it with, it will be a success. I have incorporated my favourite spices into this recipe and, being Iranian, have found a way to add pomegranate. I'm pleased to say that it works a treat!

SERVES 4–6

✳

1 whole duck, about 2–2.5kg

2 teaspoons ground coriander

2 teaspoons ground cumin

1 teaspoon ground cinnamon

1 teaspoon sumac

1 teaspoon turmeric

1 teaspoon garlic granules

1 cucumber

2 bunches of spring onions

400ml pomegranate molasses

100ml clear honey

24 Chinese pancakes (available from most supermarkets or Asian grocers)

400g pomegranate seeds

sea salt flakes

Preheat the oven to 190°C, Gas Mark 5. Line a large baking tray with baking paper.

Place the duck on the prepared baking tray. Combine all the dry spices and garlic granules in a bowl, then rub the mixture all over both sides of the duck, inside the cavity and all over the wings and legs until the dry-spice mixture is used up. Season well with salt. Roast for 2½ hours. Do not baste the duck during this time as you want to keep the skin as dry and crispy as possible.

Meanwhile, cut the cucumber into long, thin strips that are the length of a matchstick and with a thickness of about 7mm. Discard the majority of the green ends of the spring onions, then halve the white parts and slice thinly lengthways until you have lots of thin, matchstick-sized strips.

After the cooking time has elapsed, increase the oven temperature to 220°C, Gas Mark 7, and cook the duck for a further 20 minutes.

In a small saucepan set over a gentle heat, combine the pomegranate molasses with the clear honey until the mixture begins to bubble, then take the pan off the heat, stir well and set aside.

Remove the duck from the oven, cover it loosely with a sheet of kitchen foil and allow to rest for 10 minutes. Meanwhile, heat the pancakes according to the packet instructions.

To serve, plate up all the components separately (the sauce, the spring onion and cucumber strips, the pomegranate seeds and the pancakes) then, using 2 forks, shred the duck at the table. To eat, fill a pancake with some duck meat and crispy skin, some vegetable strips and a few pomegranate seeds, drizzle over a good helping of the sauce, roll up the pancake and enjoy.

KOFTA BURGERS

I have always made burgers slightly differently to those of the West. The Western technique relies on gently compressing the meat, whereas the Middle Eastern method dictates that we work the mixture thoroughly, breaking down the proteins until smooth. Not to say that one version is better than the other, but this version makes a nice change from the norm. I like my burger without cheese, but of course you can add any cheese you like, and if you want to something different, try a slice of grilled halloumi or some crumbled feta cheese.

MAKES 4

✳

500g minced beef (ideally 20 per cent fat)

20g fresh coriander, leaves finely chopped

1 bunch of spring onions, thinly sliced

2 heaped teaspoons garlic granules

2 heaped teaspoons ground coriander

2 teaspoons turmeric

1 teaspoon smoked paprika

2 large eggs

vegetable oil, for frying

4 burger buns (I use brioche buns), split

To serve

tomato slices

lettuce leaves

sliced pickles

raw sliced red onion rings

ketchup

mayonnaise

Heat 2 large frying pans over a medium heat.

Combine the beef, fresh coriander, spring onions, garlic granules, spices and eggs in a mixing bowl and mix well. You really need to work the mixture very well into a smooth, evenly combined paste. Divide the mixture into 4 equal portions. Roll each portion into a ball and flatten it to make a patty.

Add a drizzle of oil to 1 pan and fry the patties for about 8 minutes (or so) on each side or until a nice crust has formed and they are cooked through. Meanwhile, toast the buns in the dry pan on the cut sides only. Serve the burgers on the base of the buns and add your favourite accompaniments.

STUFFED PEPPERS

with Rice & Beef

Mama G, a wonderful cook and the mother of my good friend Dimitra, taught me this recipe. Every time I would visit them in Greece, she would prepare a veritable feast for us all and would always be happy to teach me how each dish was made. These stuffed peppers may seem a bit retro for our tastes today, but they are still every bit as delicious as I remember. Most countries in the Middle East have a stuffed pepper dish, so as far as I'm concerned, it's high time they came back into fashion, as they are a complete meal in themselves and colourful and versatile, too. I've added a few extra bits to the recipe and, of course, you can too.

MAKES 8

*

8 peppers (any colour you like)

olive oil, for frying and drizzling

1 large onion, finely chopped

250g lean minced beef

3 large garlic cloves, crushed

1 heaped teaspoon dried oregano

3 ripe tomatoes, cut into rough chunks

400g can chopped tomatoes

3 tablespoons tomato purée

20g flat leaf parsley, leaves and stems finely chopped

150g basmati rice

4–6 dates, pitted and finely chopped

handful of toasted pine nuts

sea salt flakes and freshly ground black pepper

Cut off the top 2.5cm of the peppers to make lids. Clean out the insides of the peppers carefully, trying not to damage or break the peppers. Ensure the lids are also intact so that they will be a tight seal when you place them back on to the peppers – this will help create steam inside for the rice to cook properly.

Heat a large frying pan over a medium-high heat. Pour enough olive oil into the hot pan to coat the base, then fry the onion until lightly golden brown. Add the mince, breaking it down as it goes in without trying to cook it, quickly followed by the crushed garlic, oregano, chopped fresh and canned tomatoes and the tomato purée and stir well. Ordinarily, you would always brown the meat first before adding other ingredients but, in this case, you want the meat to stew and remain soft, rather than become browned and firm at this stage. Ensure you stir the mixture really well to combine all the ingredients thoroughly. Season generously (in fact, over-season, as you will be adding rice to this mixture later) with salt and pepper, then take the pan off the heat and stir in the chopped parsley. Set aside to cool.

Preheat the oven to 200°C, Gas Mark 6. Line a large oven tray with a sheet of kitchen foil.

Stir the uncooked basmati rice, dates and pine nuts into the meat mixture, add a drizzle of olive oil and stir well until the mixture is evenly combined.

Stuff the peppers, filling them with the mixture two-thirds of the way to the top, leaving a good 2.5cm clear at the top of each pepper (you may have leftover stuffing if your peppers are small). Place the lid on each pepper, sit them upright on the prepared baking tray and drizzle with olive oil. Sprinkle a few handfuls of cold water on top, then roast for 45–50 minutes. Serve immediately.

SEARED STEAK
with Roasted Vegetables, Whey Dressing & Pepper Sauce

Colourful, delicious and full of flavour, this is one of those recipes that makes the key ingredient – steak, in this case – go so much further. Italians cut steak into strips and call it tagliata (*tagliata di manzo*, when using beef) and serve it up on great big platters for everyone to share. Not only does it taste delicious, but the meat stretches to feed a lot of bodies and souls, so it's a win-win situation. Roasted vegetables topped off with a tasty whey sauce take the dish to a new level.

SERVES 4–6

✳

olive oil

1 teaspoon rose harissa

600g sirloin steak or use skirt steak or onglet, if preferred

300g mixed sweet baby peppers or 2 large red, orange or yellow peppers

4 courgettes (I used 2 yellow and 2 green)

3 small red onions

5 tablespoons garlic oil

3 teaspoons dried marjoram, plus extra for sprinkling

finely grated zest and juice of 2 unwaxed lemons

6 tablespoons whey

6 tablespoons Greek yogurt

200g (drained weight) roasted red peppers (from a jar), blitzed until smooth

a few generous handfuls of rocket leaves

50g toasted pine nuts

sea salt flakes and freshly ground black pepper

Preheat the oven on a fan assisted setting to the maximum temperature. Line the largest baking tray you can find with baking paper.

Rub a little olive oil, the harissa and some black pepper over your sirloin steaks and set aside.

Halve the sweet baby peppers or, if using normal-sized large peppers, cut each into 4 strips from root to tip. Cut the courgettes diagonally across into 2.5cm-thick slices. Quarter the red onions. Put the prepared vegetables into a large mixing bowl. Add the garlic oil, marjoram, lemon zest, juice of ½ lemon, 3 generous pinches of salt and some pepper and mix well with your hands to ensure every vegetable piece is coated.

Put the whey, remaining lemon juice and yogurt in a small bowl and blend with enough olive oil until it is smooth and a sauce-like consistency. Season well with salt and pepper and set aside. Season the blitzed red pepper sauce with salt and pepper, drizzle in a little more olive oil and mix again. Set aside.

Put the courgettes and peppers (skin-sides up) on to the prepared baking tray, distributing them evenly across the pan. Drizzle the oil and lemon juice mixture they have been marinating in over the vegetables and roast for 16–18 minutes or until the vegetables are charred and cooked through.

Heat a large heavy-based frying pan over a medium-high heat until smoking hot. Sear the steaks for 4–6 minutes on each side, depending on their thickness and whether you like your steak rare or well cooked. To tell if they are still rare, poke them – if they still have a lot of bounce, they are lovely and rare inside. Once cooked on both sides, remove the steaks from the heat. They will be charred and slightly blackened on the outside as the harissa will have burned somewhat, but that's good for flavour so don't worry. Cover the steaks loosely with a sheet of kitchen foil and leave to rest for 5 minutes, then cut widthways into thin strips.

Arrange the beef and vegetables, along with the rocket leaves, on a plate. Drizzle over the whey dressing, then the red pepper sauce. Scatter over the pine nuts and some extra marjoram and serve.

LAMB, CARROT & CUMIN RICE

Inspired by my love of Afghani cuisine, this is my version of a dish an uncle's mum used to make for me when I was a kid. Her version didn't have carrots in it, but Afghani versions always do and I rather like the addition. Serve with cooling, thick Greek yogurt and a selection of pickles.

SERVES 6

∗

vegetable oil, for frying

1 large onion, thinly sliced into half moons

700g lamb neck fillets, sliced 1cm-thick

2 tablespoons cumin seeds

3 teaspoons ground cinnamon

2 teaspoons turmeric

1 teaspoon ground ginger

1 teaspoon ground cumin

1 teaspoon cayenne pepper

3 large carrots, peeled and cut into batons

500g basmati rice

sea salt flakes and freshly ground black pepper

Heat a saucepan over a medium heat, pour in enough oil to coat the base and sauté the onion until brown around the edges. Add the lamb and stir. Add the cumin seeds and other dry spices and stir to evenly coat the meat in the spicy mixture. Pour in enough boiling water from a kettle to barely cover the meat, cover with a lid, reduce the temperature to low and cook for 2 hours. Remove the lid and cook for a further 30 minutes or until the meat is tender. During cooking, stir the pan from time to time and ensure the water doesn't evaporate, adding more water if necessary to prevent the meat from sticking to the base of the pan. Once cooked, remove from the heat, stir in the carrots and set aside.

Heat a large saucepan over a high heat, fill it with boiling water and add a generous handful of sea salt flakes. Add the unwashed rice (you will wash it later) and parboil for 6 minutes. Empty the parboiled rice into a colander and wash it thoroughly with cold water to ensure it is thoroughly rinsed of starch and is cold. Drain the rice well, shaking off excess moisture and leave it to stand for about 10 minutes. Put the rice into a large mixing bowl.

Rinse the pan you used for the rice and dry it. Take a large square of baking paper and scrunch it into a ball, then open it out and use it to line the base and sides of your pan to prevent the rice from sticking. Drizzle in enough vegetable oil to generously coat the base of the pan and season the oil with some salt.

Add the meat and carrot mixture to the rice in the mixing bowl, season with a generous amount of sea salt flakes (I suggest 1 tablespoon, crushed) and black pepper and gently fold together until evenly combined. Gently pile the mixture into the saucepan in a mountain shape, then using the handle of the wooden spoon, stab a series of holes into the layers, piercing right the way down to the base of the pan (this allows the steam to circulate). Wrap the pan lid in a tea towel (to lock in the steam and make a tight seal), cover the pan and cook the rice over the lowest temperature possible if using gas, or a medium-low heat if using electric, for 45–60 minutes. A direct gas flame may burn the base of the rice dish – to avoid this, I would recommend you use a diffuser between the flame and the pan if you have one, in which case, double the cooking time. If you are lucky, you will get a nice crunchy crust.

PERSIAN LAMB, QUINCE & SAFFRON STEW

This stew hasn't quite hit the mainstream in Iran in the same way as others. I have a thing for quince and love to eat it however it comes, but my Persian heritage has given me a fondness for combining meat with fruit. When quince is in season, I fully embrace the fact by making this dish over and over again. Serve it with basmati rice.

SERVES 6

✳

vegetable oil, for frying

2 large onions, roughly diced

800g boneless lamb neck fillets, sliced into 2.5cm-thick pieces

1 teaspoon turmeric

2 generous pinches of saffron threads

1 teaspoon ground cinnamon

2–3 tablespoons clear honey

juice of ½ lemon

4 large quinces

150g dried yellow split peas

sea salt flakes and freshly ground black pepper

Set a large, heavy-based saucepan over a medium heat, add a little oil and the diced onions and soften the onions until translucent and cooked through. Increase the heat to high. Add the lamb and fry the meat for about 5 minutes, ensuring you keep the meat moving constantly to avoid stewing it in the pan.

Add the turmeric and ensure it coats the meat well. Then crumble in the saffron threads. Add the cinnamon, followed by the honey and lemon juice. Pour in just enough hot water from a kettle to cover the meat and season generously with salt. Reduce the heat to a simmer and cook for 1 hour, uncovered, stirring occasionally to prevent sticking. Top up with water if necessary during cooking.

Meanwhile, heat a large frying pan over a medium heat. Peel and core the quinces and cut them into halves if using smaller quince, or quarters if using larger quince. Drizzle some oil into the pan and fry the quince pieces until they are golden (not brown-black, which would taint the precious saffron-tinted colour of the stew). Once sealed on the outsides, remove the quince from the pan and set aside.

Add the yellow split peas to the saucepan containing the meat mixture, mix well and add a little more water if needed (to just cover the contents of the pan). Cook for 1 hour. Remove the pan from heat, check the seasoning and adjust as necessary, then gently place the cooked quince on top of the stew. Put on the saucepan lid, shake the pot a little to allow the quince pieces to naturally sink into the pan, and continue cooking for a further 30 minutes.

LAMB, SAFFRON, DRIED LIME & CUMIN-SPICED RICE

Given the risk of offending Spanish folk everywhere, I cannot call this dish a paella as I use basmati rice, lamb and quite a few non-traditional ingredients. My friend, the Spanish chef Omar Allibhoy, invented a Persian-inspired paella for a collaboration we did together. I loved it so much that I had to pay homage with this simple version.

SERVES 6

✳

olive oil, for frying

2 onions, finely chopped

800g lamb neck fillet, cut into
2.5cm-thick slices

2 heaped teaspoons turmeric

6 garlic cloves, thinly sliced

1 large red pepper, halved lengthways
deseeded and cut into 5mm strips

500g basmati rice

4 teaspoons ground cumin

4 teaspoons dried lime powder
(or grind dried limes, if preferred)

1g (a small pinch) saffron threads

2 litres good vegetable or chicken stock
or water (if using stock cubes, omit
the salt)

150g fresh or frozen peas

sea salt flakes and freshly ground
black pepper

lemon wedges, to serve

Heat a saucepan over a medium heat, add enough olive oil to coat the base of the pan and fry half the chopped onions until they begin to soften and colour around the edges. Add the lamb and stir. Next, add the turmeric and a generous amount of salt and pepper and mix well before covering the lamb with just enough hot water from a kettle to almost cover the lamb. Stir again, reduce the heat to low, cover the saucepan with a lid and simmer for 2 hours or until the meat is soft and cooked through. Check the volume of liquid every 30 minutes or so to ensure the pan doesn't dry out and add more hot water only if necessary. After 2 hours, remove from the heat and set aside.

Select a large, deep frying pan, a paella pan or a shallow casserole, place it on a medium-high heat and drizzle in a generous amount of olive oil. Fry the remaining onions until they begin to turn golden brown. Add the garlic slices and keep stirring to prevent them from burning. Next, add the pepper strips, followed by the dry basmati rice (and a little more oil, if needed) and 'toast' the rice in the pan stirring constantly without colouring or burning it. Add the cumin, dried lime and a generous amount of salt and pepper, then crumble in the saffron threads, making the powder as fine as possible. Stir well. You can always add a little more oil or water if needed to prevent the mixture from sticking.

Add the lamb and its juices to the pan, pour in the stock or water and stir, then add the peas. Cover the saucepan and cook for 10 minutes, then reduce the heat to low and cook for a further 15–20 minutes or until the rice is cooked. Once done, take the pan off the heat and allow the dish to rest for 5 minutes. Serve with lemon wedges.

SIX-HOUR EASTERN-SPICED PORK BELLY

Slow-cooked meat is a thing of beauty, and you can often transform a simple, inexpensive cut of meat into something really special. Pork belly has a high fat content, which helps to keep it delicious and moist throughout cooking, while the crackling is nothing short of spectacular when done well. Middle Eastern spices work wonders with pork belly and the addition of flavour to both the crackling and the meat really give this dish something extra. Leftovers – if there are any – make superb sandwiches.

SERVES 6

✳

1.5kg pork belly

4–5 tablespoons garlic oil

2 teaspoons ground coriander

2 teaspoons garlic powder

2 teaspoons ground ginger

1 teaspoon ground sweet paprika

1 teaspoon ground cumin

1 teaspoon turmeric

5 green cardamom pods, cracked

3 black cardamom pods

1 finger-sized piece of cinnamon bark (not cinnamon sticks)

175ml cloudy apple juice

juice of 2 oranges

3 heaped teaspoons sea salt flakes, crushed

175ml water

Preheat the oven to 150°C, Gas Mark 2. Line a large baking tray with baking paper.

Score the fat on the top of the pork belly in strips about 1cm apart. Rub the garlic oil all over the pork belly.

In a small bowl, combine the ground coriander, garlic powder, ginger, paprika, cumin and turmeric and work the spice rub all over the meat. Place the joint on to the prepared baking tray. Add the green and black cardamom pods and the cinnamon bark into the baking tray along with the apple and orange juices and half the crushed sea salt flakes, then pour in the 175ml of water up to where the fat begins (some pork bellies are taller than others so you may not need all the liquid). Sprinkle the remaining salt on top of the pork and rub it in. Roast, without basting, for 5½ hours (don't be tempted to baste it, as you won't get crispy crackling if you do). Top up with water if necessary.

Increase the oven temperature to 240°C, Gas Mark 9, and roast for a further 30 minutes or until the pork belly is deep brown and crispy. Remove from the oven, cover loosely with kitchen foil and leave to rest for 10 minutes before slicing and serving.

STIR-FRIED TANGY PRAWNS

Prawns are really useful to keep in the freezer for emergencies – they can be cooked in a blink and in myriad ways, helping you to make a meal out of simple ingredients in minutes. Traditionally in Iran, you eat seafood only if you live near the sea. My grandma used to call prawns *joonevar* (Farsi for 'insects') because of their appearance when whole, and would never eat them, but I love them in all their shapes and sizes. They always make a dish feel special. I love eating this dish with rice, but you can serve it with bread or any grain you like.

SERVES 4

✳

vegetable oil

2 large onions, thinly sliced into half moons

7.5cm piece of fresh root ginger, peeled and cut into matchsticks

1 large garlic bulb, cloves peeled and roughly sliced

3–4 lime leaves, rolled and thinly sliced into ribbons

6 red pickled chillies, thinly sliced

1 teaspoon fenugreek seeds

4 cardamom pods, lightly crushed

2 teaspoons turmeric

1 teaspoon ground cinnamon

400–600g raw tiger prawns, peeled but with tails left on

6 preserved lemons, halved, deseeded and sliced into half moons

½ cucumber, peeled, halved lengthways, deseeded and cut into 1cm slices

50g fresh coriander, leaves and stems roughly chopped

sea salt flakes and freshly ground black pepper

If you have a wok, heat it over a high heat. Otherwise, heat a large saucepan over a high heat.

Pour a generous amount of oil into the pan and, once it is hot, fry the onions, stirring only occasionally to prevent burning, until golden brown and crispy. Then, working quickly, add the ginger, garlic, lime leaves, chilli and the spices and keep stirring the mixture to prevent burning. Now add the prawns and coat them in the mixture well. Stir-fry for 1 minute (or more, if they are large), then add the preserved lemons and stir-fry for about 1 minute more or so or until some of the juices have evaporated. Add the cucumber slices, stir and, finally, add the chopped coriander. Stir-fry the mixture for 2 minutes until the prawns turn pink and are cooked through, then serve immediately.

HARISSA MUSSELS

Mussels hold their own wonderfully in so many dishes, from risottos and paellas to pies and pastas, and work well with many different flavours. The first time I ever ate them was in Paris – moules marinière with French fries – what a perfect combination. I've been hooked on them ever since. I have tried many different flavourings with mussels, from Italian and Thai to Caribbean and Spanish, and every single time my favourite versions include chilli, so – naturally – a version with harissa had to be on the horizon. This dish is nicely spicy, and with a hunk of crusty bread to mop up the juices, it's a total winner.

SERVES 2–4

✳

olive oil, for frying

50g salted butter

1 large onion, halved and sliced into half moons

6 fat garlic cloves, thinly sliced

2 heaped teaspoons rose harissa

1kg mussels, cleaned and beards removed

300ml white wine

1 heaped teaspoon clear honey

1 tablespoon sea salt flakes

½ small packet (about 15g) of dill, fronds finely chopped

You'll need a saucepan that's large enough to fit all the mussels. Heat it up over a high heat.

Drizzle in enough olive oil to coat the base of the pan, add the butter and onion and fry the onion until just beginning to colour. Add the garlic and stir constantly to avoid burning it. Mix in the harissa, then add the mussels and coat them in the spicy mixture as best you can. Stir in the wine, honey and salt, mixing well. Cover the saucepan with a lid and allow the mussels to open and cook through. This should take no more than 5 minutes.

Remove the lid, give the mussels a good stir and discard any unopened ones. Mix in the chopped dill and serve.

TURMERIC CLAM STIR-FRY

My love affair with clams began when I was served my first plate of *spaghetti alle vongole*. This straightforward recipe requires such little effort, but you're rewarded with so much flavour. The delicious taste of fresh turmeric is much more delicate and complex than ground turmeric. Once you start using fresh turmeric, you'll want to add it into more and more of your dishes at home, as it is a highly versatile ingredient. Serve this ideally with fresh, crusty baguette.

SERVES 4

✳

50g fresh turmeric root, thinly sliced (no need to peel)

2 long red chillies, finely chopped

50g fresh coriander, leaves roughly chopped

olive oil, for frying

8 garlic cloves, thinly sliced

1kg small clams, washed

sea salt flakes

Using a pestle and mortar, grind the turmeric slices, chillies and coriander with a couple of pinches of salt to a coarse paste. Don't worry if it's not totally smooth, as it really doesn't have to be – just ensure you have mashed up the turmeric so there are no whole slices left.

Set a large pan over a medium-high heat, drizzle in enough oil to lightly coat the base of the pan, then add the garlic and cook until the edges begin to turn golden. Add the paste (and a little more oil, if needed) and stir-fry the paste, cooking out the ingredients without burning the mixture. Then add the clams, stir well to coat the clams with the paste, cover the pan with a lid and cook for 5–6 minutes or until the clams open. Remove the lid (there should be a nice amount of liquid in the pan), taste and add more salt if desired, then baste the clams a few times with the liquid and discard any unopened clams before serving.

CHARGRILLED OCTOPUS
with Maple Chilli Dressing & Pistachios

Eating octopus always reminds me of being on holiday in Spain or Greece. When cooked well, it can be one of my favourite things to eat – I always order it if I see it on a menu. People are often squeamish about cooking octopus but, rest assured, it is incredibly easy and the results are very rewarding. Just expect about 30–40 per cent shrinkage when cooking. Delicious, meltingly tender bites of octopus are even better if chargrilled or finished on the barbecue. This is my humble homemade version.

SERVES 4

✳

2kg octopus (I prefer just tentacles from a large octopus,
    rather than whole small ones)
3 heaped teaspoons rose harissa
5 tablespoons maple syrup
olive oil, for drizzling
50g pistachio slivers or 75g pistachios, chopped (skin on is fine)
sea salt flakes

Bring a large saucepan of generously salted water to the boil, add the octopus, reduce the heat to medium-low immediately and simmer for 2 hours or, if using a whole octopus, for 3 hours. Drain and plunge the octopus into cold water.

In a small saucepan, combine the harissa and maple syrup and heat gently. As soon as the mixture begins to bubble, take the pan off the heat and set aside.

Heat a griddle pan or a heavy-based saucepan over a high heat. Dry the octopus pieces using kitchen paper (don't worry if some of the skin begins to rub away) and cut them into manageable lengths that will easily fit on to your griddle pan. Rub all the octopus pieces with olive oil to coat them well. Cooking in batches, sear the octopus on the hot griddle for 1–2 minutes (depending on the size of the pieces) or until char marks appear. Transfer to a plate.

Slice the octopus according to your preference and arrange on a serving plate. Drizzle the sauce liberally over the octopus slices, drizzle with a little olive oil and scatter over the pistachios to finish.

CHARGRILLED SQUID
with Grapefruit, Herbs & Pomegranate Seeds

I hated squid until I was in my late twenties. I'm not sure what changed, but I am fairly confident in the assertion that I have eaten the equivalent of my body weight in squid since my conversion. Chargrilling and deep-frying are my favourite ways to cook squid and I always keep some baby squid in my freezer for emergencies, as it can be used to enliven many a meal – you can add it to salads, stir-fries and pastas. This dish is so refreshing and, in the depths of winter, it provides a vibrant, zingy taste of summer, bursting with flavour and juicy sweetness.

SERVES 4
✳

500g baby squid, cleaned and sliced into rings
olive oil, for drizzling
2 teaspoons pul biber chilli flakes
1 large grapefruit (I use ruby red)
20g mint, leaves roughly chopped
20g chives, snipped into 1cm strips
20g chervil (or use coriander), leaves roughly chopped
150g pomegranate seeds
sea salt flakes and freshly ground black pepper

Preheat a griddle pan or heavy-based frying pan over a medium-high heat.

Place the squid in a bowl, drizzle generously with olive oil, add the chilli flakes and a very generous seasoning of black pepper and mix well.

You'll need a sharp knife to peel the grapefruit. Cut off the top and base of the grapefruit, then cut away the remaining peel and pith in strips until the entire grapefruit is peeled. Cut the grapefruit in half lengthways, then cut slices about 5mm thick. Now cut each slice into 3 segments and place in a mixing bowl.

Place the squid on the hot griddle pan and spread them out. Cook without moving for 1–2 minutes or until the undersides begin to char, then quickly turn over the pieces and cook for a further minute. Transfer to a plate and leave to cool for a few minutes.

Put the cooled squid into the bowl with the grapefruit pieces. Season generously with salt, add a drizzle of olive oil and mix well to coat. Add the fresh herbs and pomegranate seeds, mix well and serve immediately.

EASTERN-STYLE FISH & CHIPS

I discovered the joys of proper fish and chips on my first day at secondary school aged 11. One of my friends took me to the local chippy after school and introduced me to a newspaper-wrapped parcel of fried goodness that won me over in an instant. I even became a malt vinegar convert that day. There are no chip shops anywhere near me now, so if I want really good fish and chips, I have to make my own. I have made so many different versions with every kind of batter or crumb imaginable, but I like this particular method the best.

SERVES 3–4

*

approximately 750ml vegetable oil

2 large eggs, beaten

100g plain flour

2 teaspoons sweet paprika

2 teaspoons English mustard powder

3 teaspoons ground coriander

1 teaspoon turmeric

1 teaspoon cayenne pepper

600g cod fillets (or any thick white fish), cut into 8 portions

sea salt flakes and black pepper

ketchup, to serve

For the chips

750ml vegetable oil

1–1.5kg floury potatoes (unpeeled), cut into thin chips

Preheat 2 large saucepans or deep frying pans over a medium heat. Put the oil for cooking the chips into 1 pan, and the oil for frying the fish into the other. Bring the oil up to frying temperature, but do not allow it to smoke. Place the potatoes in 1 pan and begin to cook them.

Meanwhile, put the beaten eggs into a small, shallow bowl and season with salt and pepper. Put the flour and all the spices into another shallow bowl, season generously with salt and pepper and mix until evenly combined. Coat each piece of fish evenly in the seasoned flour, shaking off any excess, then dip it into the egg mixture until fully coated, and finish by dredging it in the flour mixture again, ensuring each piece is well coated. Repeat until all the pieces are coated. Fry the fish in the second pan of oil until the batter is crispy and a deep golden brown.

Remove the chips and the fish from the oil using a metal slotted spoon and drain on kitchen paper to absorb any excess oil. Transfer to serving plates, season with salt and serve immediately with ketchup.

LEMON, TURMERIC & BLACK PEPPER SALMON

This may be literally the easiest recipe I ever came up with for salmon, yet it always delivers the wow factor. One day I was stuck for ideas for spicing up my salmon, so I raided my spice rack, added a little lemon zest and this recipe was born. You can, of course, use salmon fillets, but serving up a side of salmon prepared in this way makes it really impressive.

SERVES 6–8

✳

1kg salmon side

finely grated zest of 3 unwaxed lemons

1 tablespoon coarse black pepper

4 tablespoons garlic oil

2 tablespoons turmeric

1 heaped teaspoon sea salt flakes, crushed

Preheat the oven to 240°C, Gas Mark 9. Line the largest baking tray you have with baking paper.

Place the salmon side, skin-side down (if applicable), on to the prepared baking tray.

In a small bowl, make a paste using the lemon zest, coarse black pepper, garlic oil and turmeric and mix well until smooth and well combined. Rub the mixture evenly all over the exposed salmon flesh. (If desired, you can now leave the salmon in the refrigerator to marinate for 1 hour or even overnight, as long as you don't add salt to it.) Season the salmon evenly with the sea salt. Roast for 22 minutes – the flesh should still feel firm to the touch – then serve immediately.

superb bakes
&
sweet treats

DARK CHOCOLATE & PISTACHIO
COOKIES *page 218*

DATE & ORANGE CINNAMON
SCONES *page 214*

CARDAMOM DOUGHNUT
BRIOCHE FRENCH TOASTS
page 34

BLACKBERRY TART
page 216

SPICED PARSNIP, WALNUT & HONEY CAKE
with Whipped Yogurt

I love cake. I love parsnips. Combining the two is a total no-brainer for me. I've improved upon this recipe over many years because – while I'm very fond of carrot cake – if I'm honest I like parsnip cake even more. This is a very satisfying dessert that keeps well, and the whipped yogurt really rounds it off for me.

SERVES 8–10

✳

3 large eggs

200g golden caster sugar

2 teaspoons vanilla bean paste

1 heaped teaspoon ground ginger

1 heaped teaspoon ground cinnamon

3 heaped tablespoons clear honey

150g butter, melted and cooled

225g self-raising flour

300g parsnips, peeled and finely grated

150g broken walnut pieces

2 handfuls golden raisins (optional)

For the whipped yogurt

400g thick Greek yogurt

4 tablespoons icing sugar

2 teaspoons vanilla bean paste (optional)

Preheat the oven to 160°C, Gas Mark 3. Line a 24cm square cake tin with baking paper.

To make the cake, cream the eggs and sugar together in a large mixing bowl. Add the vanilla paste and spices, followed by the honey and butter and mix until evenly combined. Slowly incorporate the flour until you have a smooth batter. Finally, add the parsnips, walnut pieces and raisins (if using) and mix well again.

Pour the batter into the cake tin and bake for 1¼ hours or until deep golden brown on top. Once done, remove from the oven and allow the cake to cool completely.

To make the whipped yogurt, combine the ingredients in a mixing bowl and whip with an electric whisk for a couple of minutes or until the mixture has a consistency you like. I like it quite thick, so persevere if this is what you like. Serve the cake with a generous dollop of the whipped yogurt on the side.

DATE & ORANGE CINNAMON SCONES

The quintessential English afternoon tea is never complete without scones and clotted cream. I absolutely love the stuff. I have had my fair share of cream teas, from the classic grand afternoon teas at The Ritz, Claridge's and the Wolseley to more humble, down-to-earth tea room offerings all over England, and a good scone cannot be beaten. I like mine with dates – it seems mean to leave out a decent burst of sweetness. I often bake my own using whatever dried fruit, nuts and even savoury ingredients I need to use up.

MAKES 8–10

*

250g self-raising flour, plus extra for dusting

1 heaped teaspoon baking powder

50g salted butter, at room temperature

2 teaspoons ground cinnamon

finely grated zest of 2 unwaxed oranges

30g caster sugar

1 large egg

125ml milk, plus extra for glazing

100g large dates, pitted and roughly chopped

To serve
butter or clotted cream
honey
ground cinnamon

Preheat the oven to 200°C, Gas Mark 6. Line a baking tray with baking paper.

Put the flour and baking powder into a large bowl, then rub the butter into the flour using your fingertips until the mixture resembles breadcrumbs. Add the cinnamon, orange zest, sugar, egg, milk and dates and work the mixture into a sticky, soft dough. Sprinkle some flour on to a clean surface and roll out the dough until it is just under 2.5cm thick. Using a round pastry cutter or a small glass, stamp out as many rounds of the dough as you can and place them on the baking tray. Brush each dough circle with milk. Bake for 12–15 minutes or until the scones are nicely risen and golden brown.

Transfer to a wire rack and leave to cool before smothering with butter or clotted cream, honey and a sprinkle of cinnamon.

BLACKBERRY TART

with Pistachio Frangipane

Pastry making was never something that came naturally to me and, after conquering my fear with a little hands-on help from chef Raymond Blanc, I finally found a super-simple recipe for great shortcrust pastry that was so easy, I was embarrassed I hadn't faced my fear earlier. I went on to make dozens of different tarts using the same pastry base, but none were ever as popular as this one with good, juicy blackberries that complement the sweet pistachio frangipane more than any other fruit. But feel free to experiment with your favourite fruit and flavour combinations – this recipe works very well with poached apricots, apples, pears and so many other fruits.

MAKES 2 PASTRY CASES AND ENOUGH FILLING FOR 1 TART (SERVES 6–8)

✳

For the pastry

250g plain flour, plus extra for dusting
125g unsalted butter, at room temperature
30g caster sugar
pinch of sea salt flakes, crushed
1 egg beaten with 1 egg yolk

For the filling

50g unsalted butter, at room temperature
75g caster sugar
70g pistachio slivers or skinless kernels, finely ground
1 egg
1 heaped teaspoon vanilla bean paste
12g plain flour
200g blackberries

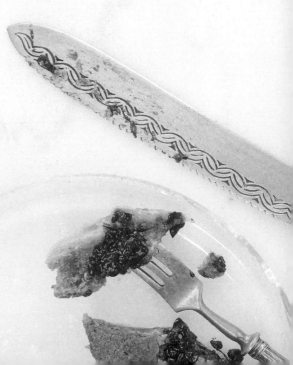

First, make the pastry. Put the flour, butter, sugar and crushed salt into a mixing bowl and use your fingertips to rub the ingredients together, lifting the flour upwards from the base of the bowl, until the mixture is combined and has a sand-like consistency. Make a well in the centre of the mixture and pour in the beaten egg. Using a fork, work the sandy mixture into the beaten egg until the mixture is even, then form into a ball.

Dust a clean surface with some flour and knead the pastry dough for about 1 minute. Then halve the dough, wrap 1 portion in clingfilm and refrigerate or freeze for another occasion. Place a large length of clingfilm on your work surface and position the remaining portion of dough in the centre. Loosely cover the pastry dough with another piece of clingfilm. Using a rolling pin, roll out the dough between the layers of clingfilm until it is a little larger than a 20cm-diameter loose-based tart or flan tin. Peel away the top sheet of clingfilm. Place your hand under the clingfilm below the pastry dough, lift it and gently drape it into the tin. Peel away the clingfilm and scrunch it up into a ball. Use this clingfilm ball to press the dough gently into the grooves of the tart tin and smooth out the base. Repair any cracks or tears using any excess overhanging dough. Once the tin is lined, press a rolling pin over the top edge of the tin, which will neatly cut away any excess pastry, leaving perfectly levelled edges all around the shell. Refrigerate for 30 minutes.

Meanwhile, make the pistachio frangipane. Mix all the ingredients except the blackberries together in a bowl until smooth and set aside. Approximately 10 minutes before your pastry case has fully chilled, preheat the oven to 180°C, Gas Mark 4.

Remove the pastry dough from the refrigerator and pour in the frangipane. Gently (without pushing them into the frangipane) place the blackberries on the surface of the filling. Bake for 45 minutes or until golden brown on top. Remove the tart from the oven and allow to cool before devouring.

DARK CHOCOLATE & PISTACHIO COOKIES

Everyone loves cookies. No matter what they are made with, they are a welcome treat for kids and grown-ups alike. Personally, I am very fussy when it comes to cookies. I don't like them too chunky, and I prefer them to be a little bit chewy but with a crisp exterior. I only like dark chocolate – but as pieces, not to flavour the entire cookie. And the addition of nuts makes the perfect cookie as far as I'm concerned. See? Fussy. So here is a recipe for my perfect cookie – delicious with a glass of cold milk. If you are equally particular about your biscuits, it's easy to change the ingredients and use nuts, fruit and chocolate according to your preferences, to produce your own version.

MAKES 14–16

✳

100g salted butter, softened

100g light brown sugar

75g caster sugar

1 large egg

1 heaped teaspoon vanilla bean paste

175g plain flour

100g pistachio slivers or chopped pistachios

150g dark chocolate chunks

Preheat the oven to 180°C, Gas Mark 4. Line a large baking tray with baking paper.

Cream the butter and sugars together in a bowl (an electric whisk does the job very well), then add the egg and vanilla paste and mix until smooth.

Add the flour and incorporate it into the creamed mixture until a dough forms. Finally, mix in the pistachios and chocolate chunks, ensuring they are evenly distributed throughout the mixture.

I like my cookies fairly large so I divide the mixture into 14–16 equal portions and roll these into 3cm balls. Place as many of the balls as you can on the prepared baking tray, ensuring you leave a space of 5cm around each ball as they will spread out a lot. Bake for 13–15 minutes or until golden at the edges. Remove from the oven and leave to cool for a few minutes, then enjoy them warm.

SPICED APPLE, ROSEMARY & PECAN MUFFINS

Muffins are so easy to make and work in both sweet and savoury versions. I am mildly obsessed with combining sweet and savoury flavours, and here I tie in the freshness of rosemary, which I think gives these muffins a unique twist. In my mind, they are absolutely perfect with a strong, mature cheese such as Cheddar. So don't think of this as a traditional sweet muffin but, instead, something for a breakfast table or an afternoon treat.

MAKES 10–12

✳

1 large egg

175g caster sugar

handful of rosemary, leaves very finely chopped

1 tablespoon vanilla bean paste

1 heaped teaspoon ground cinnamon

75g salted butter, melted and cooled slightly

finely grated zest of 1 unwaxed lemon

275g plain flour

2 heaped teaspoons baking powder

200ml milk

1 large Braeburn apple, cored and cut into 1cm dice

75g pecan nuts, halved

good handful of currants or raisins

Preheat the oven to 190°C, Gas Mark 5.

Place muffin cases into the holes of a muffin tin (unless you are using a silicone muffin tray).

In a mixing bowl, beat together the egg, sugar, rosemary, vanilla, cinnamon, butter and lemon zest.

Sift the flour and baking powder into a large bowl, add the milk and mix well until the batter is smooth. Add the egg, rosemary and cinnamon mixture along with the apples, pecans and currants or raisins and mix until all the ingredients are evenly incorporated into the batter.

Divide the mixture into the muffin cases (don't overfill them as the batter will rise) and bake for 30–35 minutes or until golden brown on top. Remove from the tin and allow to cool, then serve – and trust me on the Cheddar or mature cheese pairing (see above)!

ALMOND & CITRUS DRIZZLE LOAF

Lemon drizzle cake has to be one of my absolute favourites. I never tire of its tangy flavour and crunchy, sharp sugar topping and it really is heavenly with a lovely big cup of tea. It's no secret that I am obsessed with using the grated zest of citrus fruits, and here I've amped up the flavour by adding limes and oranges into the mix. The result is a lovely twist on a classic that's every bit as delicious.

MAKES 1

✳

2 large eggs
150g caster sugar
finely grated zest of 2 unwaxed oranges
finely grated zest of 1 unwaxed lime
finely grated zest of 1 unwaxed lemon
150g unsalted butter, softened
150g plain flour
1 teaspoon baking powder
100g ground almonds
6 tablespoons milk

For the citrus drizzle
75g granulated sugar
juice of 1 lime
juice of ½ orange

Preheat the oven to 180°C, Gas Mark 4. Line a 900g loaf tin with baking paper.

Beat the eggs, sugar, citrus zests and butter together until the mixture is evenly combined.
Add the flour, baking powder and ground almonds, followed by the milk, and mix well until smooth.
Pour the batter into the prepared loaf tin and bake for 45 minutes or until golden brown on top and a skewer when inserted comes out clean.

To make the citrus drizzle, mix the granulated sugar with the lime and orange juices.

Remove the cake from the oven and, while it is still hot, spoon the drizzle over the cake. Leave the cake to cool completely in the tin before serving.

NECTARINE PAVLOVA
with Mint, Almonds & Tea Syrup

The great thing about a pavlova is that it can be made in any shape you wish and topped with anything you like. I like to make mine in the same shape as my oven tray to make it easy to slice and serve. Alternatively you can just give everyone a spoon each and let them dig in!

SERVES 6

✳

6 large egg whites

300g caster sugar

½ teaspoon vanilla essence

1½ teaspoons white wine vinegar

3 teaspoons cornflour

For the topping

3 large or 4 small ripe nectarines, peeled and sliced

generous handful of mint leaves, finely chopped, plus extra to garnish

600ml double cream

1 tablespoon vanilla bean paste

6 tablespoons icing sugar

40g flaked almonds, toasted

For the tea syrup

2 Earl Grey/Darjeeling/Assam tea bags or 2 tablespoons of your favourite tea blend

250ml boiling water

6 tablespoons caster sugar

Preheat the oven to 180°C, Gas Mark 4. Line the largest oven tray you have with baking paper.

In a large, clean mixing bowl, beat the egg whites using an electric hand whisk until they form soft peaks. Slowly incorporate the caster sugar a little at a time and continue whisking until it has all been incorporated and the mixture is thick, glossy and forms stiff peaks. Add the vanilla essence, vinegar and cornflour and fold in gently (do not beat) using a spatula until evenly combined. Empty the mixture on to the prepared oven tray, shape into a rectangle and smooth the surface over with the spatula. Place in the oven and immediately lower the oven temperature to 120°C, Gas Mark ½, and bake for 1 hour.

After an hour, turn the oven off completely, but leave the meringue inside the oven as it cools (this usually takes a couple of hours).

In a small bowl, combine the sliced nectarines with the chopped mint and set aside.

To make the tea syrup, place the tea bags/leaves in a jug with the boiling water and allow to brew for 3–4 minutes, stirring well, then strain into a small saucepan. Stir in the caster sugar, then place the pan over a medium-high heat and reduce the liquid to a syrup – this will take 10–15 minutes or so.

Whip the double cream with the vanilla paste and the icing sugar until firm. Spread the cream on to the meringue, arrange the nectarines on top, drizzle the tea syrup over and sprinkle with toasted almonds and extra chopped mint to serve.

DARK CHOCOLATE, CARDAMOM & ESPRESSO MOUSSE CAKE

I don't really need to tell you how good chocolate cake is, nor shall I go on about how incredible chocolate mousse is. But put the two together and add a little spice in a simple, foolproof recipe? That's when you know you are on to a really good thing. I never get tired of making this, and because it is so light it's often my first choice of chocolate dessert to serve after one of my feasts. Serve by itself or with a scoop of vanilla bean ice cream.

SERVES 8–10
＊

200g best-quality dark chocolate
175ml olive oil
3 shots of strong espresso
seeds from 8 green cardamom pods, ground using a pestle and mortar
5 eggs, separated
75g caster sugar

Preheat the oven to 200°C, Gas Mark 6. Line a 24cm-diameter springform cake tin with baking paper.

Melt the chocolate in a heatproof bowl set over a pan of hot water, then stir in the olive oil until the mixture is smooth and fully combined. Take the bowl off the heat and leave the mixture to cool for 15 minutes. Once cool, add the espresso and ground cardamom and stir well.

Whisk the egg yolks and sugar until the mixture is pale in colour and nice and fluffy. Stir in the cooled chocolate and oil mixture.

In a separate bowl, whisk the egg whites until they reach the stiff-peak stage. Gently fold the beaten egg whites into the chocolate mixture until evenly combined.

Pour the cake mixture into the prepared tin and bake for 15 minutes. Remove from the oven and allow to cool in the tin before serving. Note that the cake will collapse slightly around the edges, but this is perfectly normal.

LIME & BASIL CREAM

with Persimmon & Black Pepper Compote

I remember as a child my mother peeling away the skin from what looked like a tomato and biting into it. I must admit that I never really liked persimmon as a child as the ripened texture was always so mushy, but as an adult I have endless appreciation for the delicate flesh and intense sweetness. Persians adore persimmon and use them to make jams and fruit leathers. This dessert is super simple to make and can be prepared in advance, so is great for entertaining. Adding a little peppery heat complements the sweet compote, which cuts beautifully through the moreish cream. If you can't find persimmons, your favourite jam will also work a treat.

MAKES 6 POTS

✳

For the persimmon & black pepper compote
2 soft and ripe persimmons
    (approximately 200g each)
75g caster sugar
finely grated zest and juice of 1 large
    unwaxed lime
1 generous teaspoon vanilla bean paste
½ teaspoon freshly ground black pepper

For the cream
900ml double cream
finely grated zest and juice of 3 large
    limes
200g caster sugar
2 handfuls of basil leaves (about 7g),
    rolled and thinly sliced into ribbons

First, prepare the cream. Put the double cream, lime zest, sugar and basil in a saucepan over a medium heat, bring to the boil, then reduce the heat to low and allow to simmer gently for 5 minutes. Add the lime juice, stir and allow to simmer for 2 minutes. Strain the mixture through a fine sieve into a measuring jug. Divide it equally into glasses, pots or little bowls and leave to cool slightly, then refrigerate for a minimum of 2 hours to set.

To make the compote, peel the persimmons carefully, ensuring you retain as much flesh as possible, and finely chop the flesh (especially the harder parts). Transfer the chopped flesh to a saucepan set over a medium-low heat. Add the sugar, lime zest and juice, vanilla bean paste and black pepper and stir the ingredients well, then cook for 45–60 minutes so that the jam is bubbling gently, not aggressively. Cooking times vary, depending on the heat source, so keep an eye on your jam and stir only 2–3 times to prevent sticking. Once it has reached a thick, jam-like consistency, remove from heat and allow to cool.

About 15 minutes before you are ready to serve, remove the cream pots from the refrigerator, divide the compote equally between them, allow to rest for 15 minutes, then serve.

QUINCE TATIN
with Cinnamon Cream

Whether this can actually be called a tarte Tatin or not, I'm not entirely sure, but the method is pretty much the same except that I use quinces instead of apples. Quinces are the apple of the Middle East, and I think they make a great alternative in desserts in which apples usually feature. The beauty of quinces is in their acidity. You can sweeten them, but you are still left with a wonderful sour wash of flavour with every bite. Another deviation from the traditional Tatin is that I use puff pastry instead of shortcrust pastry, as I find its lighter, flakier nature more enjoyable. You can make this in advance and leave in the pan to set – when you're ready to serve simply reheat in a hot oven for 5 minutes before turning out.

SERVES 6

✳

150g golden caster sugar

seeds from 1 vanilla pod

4 large quinces, peeled, cored and cut
    into wedges

75g unsalted butter, cubed

500g block ready-made puff pastry

For the cinnamon cream

300ml double cream

3 teaspoons ground cinnamon

4 tablespoons icing sugar

Preheat the oven to 200°C, Gas Mark 6.

Put the sugar in a large skillet or ovenproof frying pan over medium heat. Swirl the sugar around in the pan (don't stir) until it has dissolved and turns a deep caramel colour. Add the vanilla seeds and swirl to distribute, then add the quince wedges, cramming them into the pan as best you can. Cook for a few minutes on all sides or until they start to caramelize, then add the butter cubes around the quince and continue to cook until the quince has caramelized on all sides. Shake the pan occasionally to prevent sticking. This process should take 8–10 minutes.

If you haven't used an ovenproof frying pan, select an ovenproof dish of any shape (not too large). Carefully tip in the quince wedges (ideally, with the most caramelized sides facing down), then pour any excess caramel on top (the caramelized sugar will be extremely hot so be very careful).

Roll out the pastry to a circle just bigger than the size of your skillet/frying pan. Drape the pastry over the quince and tuck the pastry edges inside the skillet/frying pan (mind your fingers on the hot caramel). Bake on the top shelf of the oven for 25–30 minutes or until the pastry has risen and is golden brown.

Meanwhile, whip the double cream, cinnamon and icing sugar together using an electric hand whisk until fairly stiff. Keep refrigerated until ready to serve.

When cooked, remove the Tatin from the oven and leave to rest for 2 minutes. Select a serving plate or tray that is large enough to cover your skillet/frying pan. Using oven gloves or tea towels to protect your hands from the heat, cover the top of the skillet/frying pan with the plate and carefully flip over on to the serving plate (it will be runny and very hot). Serve with the cinnamon cream.

HONEY & SPICE CHALLAH

My friend Carrie from New York shared her recipe for challah with me a decade ago and the result was so good I've been making it ever since. Any stale or leftover challah can be used to make French toast (see my recipe on pages 34–5) or even bread-and-butter pudding. Its soft, doughy consistency makes it incredibly moreish, and while I love the plain recipe, here's a spiced version for those wanting something a little different.

MAKES 1 LARGE LOAF OR 2 REGULAR LOAVES

*

7g sachet fast-action dried yeast

415ml lukewarm water

3 large eggs

150ml clear honey

1 teaspoon salt

75ml unsalted butter, melted

3 heaped teaspoons ground cinnamon

1 teaspoon ground nutmeg

3 heaped teaspoons pul biber chilli flakes

800g plain flour, plus extra for dusting

butter or oil, for greasing

1 teaspoon poppy or sesame seeds

Add the yeast to 50ml of the lukewarm water, stirring well until dissolved, then set aside.

In a large mixing bowl, combine 2 of the eggs with the honey, the remaining lukewarm water, the salt and butter and whisk well until evenly mixed. Add the cinnamon, nutmeg and pul biber and blend these into the egg mixture. Now add the yeast mixture, followed by the flour. Using a wooden spoon, incorporate the flour into the liquid, using your hands at the end to ensure all the flour has been incorporated and you have a nice ball of dough. Cover the bowl with a clean tea towel and leave to rest at room temperature for 2 hours until the dough has risen.

Butter or lightly oil a large baking sheet or line with greased baking paper. Divide the dough into 2 equal portions (or keep whole to make one very large loaf as pictured opposite, but you will need a wide range oven and tray for this). Take one of the dough portions and divide it into 3 equal pieces. Dust your work surface with flour and stretch and roll each of the 3 dough pieces to form long, rope-like lengths. Pinch the 3 ends together until they join securely and carefully plait the lengths and pinch at the other end to join securely. Repeat with the second piece of dough. Carefully slide the plaited dough on to your baking sheet (this is where the extra flour you added to your work surface will be helpful) and allow to rest for a further 45 minutes.

Approximately 20 minutes before baking, preheat the oven to 200°C, Gas Mark 6.

Beat the remaining egg and brush the dough with the egg wash. Sprinkle with poppy or sesame seeds. Bake for 25–30 minutes or until the top is golden brown. Leave to cool.

INDEX

ACKNOWLEDGEMENTS

＊

I would like to thank a whole bunch of people who have now become like family to me.
Firstly to my agent Martine Carter of Sauce Management who I literally couldn't do anything without…not just my agent, but now a much loved friend and confidante, and to lovely Mimi who works with her and deals with all my panics and endless questions. To Stephanie Jackson, my publisher at Octopus, who essentially isn't just my publisher and takes way too many of my calls (especially when I panic) and who I couldn't have formulated *Sirocco* without. To Caroline Brown, Head of Publicity & Marketing who is nothing short of a magician in so many respects…I can't find enough ways to thank you for all you do and have done for me. To my brilliant creative team, incredible photographers Liz and Max Haarala Hamilton and talented food stylist Kat Mead who I count as close friends and who make the intensive shoot process full of fun, giggles, endless coffees and even more Boursin-smothered bagels. To Sybella Stephens, Jazzy Fizzle, Jonathan Christie and Pete Hunt for all your hard work on turning my garble of words into an actual book to be proud of. Thank you to Alison Goff and Denise Bates for always making me feel like a valued part of the Octopus family, and a big huge thank you to Kevin Hawkins and everyone at Octopus who put so much effort into selling, promoting, distributing and supporting my books.

A huge thank you to George Bennell at Belazu whose products continue to inspire me every day, and to everyone at Natoora for always supporting me in everything I do. Thank you also to Natalie from I.O. Shen who has always been a wonderful support and whose knives I can't work without.

Last, but not least, once again, thank you to my lovely Mum. You put up with so much crap, drama and chaos from me. I hope it has all been worth it and I hope I continue to do you proud for years to come. Love you lots Mugsy. I'm very lucky to have a mother who I can also call my best friend.

＊

The publisher would like to thank the following for their kind loan of props:
Le Creuset UK www.lecreuset.co.uk
Fired Earth www.firedearth.com
Sigmar London www.sigmarlondon.com

＊

Publishing Director: Stephanie Jackson
Managing Editor: Sybella Stephens
Copy Editor: Salima Hirani
Photographers & Prop Stylists: Haarala Hamilton Photography
Creative Director: Jonathan Christie
Designer: Jaz Bahra
Illustrator: Kim Marsland
Home Economists: Sabrina Ghayour & Kat Mead
Food Stylist: Kat Mead
Senior Production Manager: Peter Hunt